Bill Hybels is one of the most dynamic Christian leaders of our time and packs tremendous leadership wisdom into these energizing, easy-to-read essays. Don't miss them!

—Ken Blanchard, coauthor of
The One-Minute Entrepreneur™ and *Lead Like Jesus*

This is one of the most practical books I have read in years—down to earth, easy to understand, great lessons about leadership. I've ordered twenty copies for my own team.

—Chuck Colson, founder, Prison Fellowship

Leadership Axioms is a wonderful collection of insight and wisdom coming from a man who has "been there and done that." Keep it handy, read a little every day. And then read it again!

—Patrick Lencioni, president, The Table Group,
and author of *The Five Dysfunctions of a Team*

Leadership Axioms is vintage Hybels. Profound. Practical. Portable. You and your entire team are going to love this book!

—Andy Stanley, senior pastor, North Point Community Church

In this wisdom-rich book, Bill Hybels offers us not his technology, which arrives and flees as the trends go, but his *cardiology*—the heart of the matter that rests far beneath the surface. Regardless who you are, regardless where you lead, you'll find this work profound.

—Bob Roberts, author of *Transformation, Glocalization*,
and *The Multiplying Church*

Bill Hybels's *Leadership Axioms* has it all for the leader: time-tested wisdom, a-ha moments, and *serious* encouragement to persevere in the race.

—Dr. John Townsend, coauthor of *Boundaries*

In his insightful book *Leadership Axioms*, Hybels paints a much-needed picture of true success.

—Eleanor Josaitis, cofounder, Focus: HOPE

When it comes to leadership wisdom, Bill Hybels hits it out of the park. I read *Leadership Axioms* in one sitting but will reflect on it for years.

—Larry Osborne, author and pastor, North Coast Church, Vista, Calif.

Books by Bill Hybels

Holy Discontent

Just Walk Across the Room

The Volunteer Revolution

Courageous Leadership

Too Busy Not to Pray

Honest to God?

Fit to Be Tied
(with Lynne Hybels)

Descending into Greatness
(with Rob Wilkins)

Becoming a Contagious Christian
(with Mark Mittelberg and Lee Strobel)

The New Community Series
(with Kevin and Sherry Harney)

Colossians

James

1 Peter

Philippians

Romans

The Sermon on the Mount 1

The Sermon on the Mount 2

The InterActions Small Group Series
(with Kevin and Sherry Harney)

Authenticity	*Love in Action*
Character	*Marriage*
Commitment	*Meeting God*
Community	*New Identity*
Essential Christianity	*Parenting*
Fruit of the Spirit	*Prayer*
Getting a Grip	*Reaching Out*
Jesus	*The Real Deal*
Lessons on Love	*Significance*
Living in God's Power	*Transformation*

Foreword by HENRY CLOUD, PhD

leadership
axioms.

POWERFUL LEADERSHIP PROVERBS

Bill Hybels

Previously published as AXIOM

 ZONDERVAN®   WILLOW
Willow Creek Resources

ZONDERVAN.com/
AUTHORTRACKER
follow your favorite authors

ZONDERVAN

Leadership Axioms
Copyright © 2008 by Bill Hybels

Previously published as *Axiom*

Requests for information should be addressed to:
Zondervan, *Grand Rapids, Michigan* 49530

This edition: ISBN 978-0-310-49596-3 (softcover)

The Library of Congress cataloged the original edition as follows:

Hybels, Bill.
    Axiom : Powerful leadership proverbs / Bill Hybels.
      p. cm.
    ISBN 978-0-310-27236-6 (hardcover, jacketed)
    1. Leadership — Religious aspects — Christianity. 2. Leadership. I. Title.
BV4597.53.L43H93 2008
253 — dc22   2008009574

Cover design: Faceout Studio
Interior design: Rob Monacelli and Ben Fetterley

Printed in the United States of America

13 14 15 16 17 18 19 20 /DCI/ 19 18 17 16 15 14 13 12 11 10 9 8 7 6 5

FOR THE LAST TWENTY YEARS,
I have had the extraordinary privilege to work
alongside two of the most capable leaders in
the kingdom: one, a Stanford grad from Texas
who wears boots to operas, prepares gourmet
meals, and demonstrates to his sons how to
sack opposing quarterbacks in the park district
football league. The other, a Harvard grad who
coaches a girls' pole-vaulting team on the side
and can still high jump his own height at forty-
five years of age.

Greg Hawkins and Jim Mellado make coming
to work every day pure delight for me. Godly,
smart, humble, team-oriented — the list could
go on. Colaboring with them has been a gift
beyond what they ever could understand.

This one's for you, guys!

CONTENTS

Foreword by
Henry Cloud, PhD

We've all had the experience of going to the doctor and being told to take a pill for what ails us. It seems too small, too simple to be effective, but amazingly, once we toss back a dose or two, the pain is relieved, the infection is fought, and full-capacity functioning resurfaces once more. Behind that pill is years of research, lots of biochemical brainwork done by guys so nerdy they're denied interaction with normal people, extensive clinical trials, failures and redesigns, hundreds of millions of dollars, and proven success. In short, concealed in that innocent-looking solution is the power to change *everything*.

It's a fitting analogy because in this collection of "leadership proverbs," as Bill has termed them, you're offered a handful of powerful little pills that can either turn a sick leadership situation around or boost its immune system so that it never has to fall ill. The principles of *Leadership Axioms* are that simple and yet that profound. And like all worthwhile medicines, they are supported by years of research, rigorous trials, colossal failures and subsequent redesigns, millions of dollars, and buckets of blood, sweat, and tears. They work. And as a leadership consultant and coach to small organizations and Fortune 500 companies alike, I have witnessed firsthand what happens to a leader's three primary leadership responsibilities when principles like these are utilized ... and when they are not.

A leader's responsibility, first and foremost, is to cause a vision and mission to have tangible results in the real world. Without a *real* difference made in *real* people's lives, a vision is relegated to a pipe dream, a mission to a series of wishes posted on the wall. Great leaders—whether they labor in the marketplace or in a ministry setting—demand the achievement of results that the people being served can actually count, measure, and feel. This book will show you how to do just that.

A leader is also responsible for the experience of his or her followers. If your leadership is sound, not only are you *hitting the numbers*, but you are also *lifting the people* to experience more health, more growth, more success, and an upswing in fulfillment as a result of being on the journey with you. Great leaders cultivate an environment where instead of people getting injured, discouraged, and burned out, they are equipped to become what they never thought they could be and achieve things they never thought they could achieve. Great leaders grow not just results, but people too. This book will show you how to do that.

The leader's third responsibility — and the toughest of them all — is self-leadership, the commitment to constant improvement as a leader. Few things are more tragic than seeing zeal, talent, and a God-given goal fail because a leader neglected to get better. Many times I look at someone with all the gifts in the world and think, "If you had just understood this *one* thing, then *everything* would have turned out differently." My heart aches for how beat-up and bewildered and just plain *tired* leaders can become. Great leaders do their homework so that weariness and unsteadiness are kept at bay. They seize as many "one things" as possible so that they wind up not a leadership statistic but a leadership success. This is the gift of *Leadership Axioms*, the presentation of a whole slew of tried and true "one things."

I've seen Bill lead. I've led alongside him. And I've studied how he works. The lessons learned he offers in *Leadership Axioms* were not born in some academic think tank. They were born in the heart and soul of a real guy who started his leadership journey with nothing more than a vision, a fair amount of energy, and a boatload of faith. Today, his living legacy is impacting quite literally the face of the church around the globe. There are times when a good leadership coach will recommend a book to another leader or to a client. When I reviewed an advance copy of *Leadership Axioms*, I didn't want to recommend for my friends and clients to read it; I wanted to *require* them to do so. I want the same for you. You will be encouraged by Bill's empathy for your leadership burden. He has been in the trenches, and it shows. You will be comforted by his companionship as both trainer and friend. And you will be challenged to reach for the kinds of results that these proverbs have produced in Willow's mission, its incredible team of people and members, and in Bill himself. Get this book's principles in you. It's a simple-seeming solution, but it has the power to change everything.

— Los Angeles 2008

INTRODUCTION

Being on the road as much as I am doesn't make for a very glamorous life. But every once in a while I get to train leaders in a setting that is so stunning it makes the flight delays, filthy taxicabs, and lost baggage fade into oblivion.

Rio de Janeiro has always been such a place. I went there as a kid and have returned on several occasions since, but just this year I had the best trip there to date. My purpose in going was to train pastors and to cast vision for the Global Leadership Summit—a conference put on by the Willow Creek Association. One evening I realized I had four consecutive hours of unassigned time. This almost never happens on my kind of trips, so I grabbed my journal, a couple of books, and headed down to a sidewalk café overlooking Copacabana Beach in search of fresh fish and a glass of Brazil's "whatever." Ahhh ...

Once I'd ordered dinner, I began speed-reading *The Powell Principles*, a book high on my reading list because I was slated to interview General Colin Powell later that month. As I flipped through the first few pages, I noticed its interesting format; instead of long, drawn-out chapters, the book simply captured a couple dozen of Powell's greatest lessons learned from his days as an active-duty soldier and, later, as the chairman of the Joint Chiefs of Staff and stated them in principle form. I plowed through all twenty-four of them—each key principle offered in ten words or less—and gained passion and energy with every page. I was fascinated by the fact that for almost forty years General Powell had led according to these pithy adages—such as, "Maintain an open-door policy," "Probe the organization," and "Promote a clash of ideas."

Reading Powell's quick-stated convictions validated something I've long believed, that great leaders not only lead well but are also able to articulate in short, memorable phrases precisely how they do so. Hold that thought.

One of my favorite Old Testament books is Proverbs. I've read it dozens of times, yet it inspires me afresh with every reading. Proverbs is unique in that it serves up a truckload of weighty wisdom in bite-size chunks. You don't have to wander through a frustrating maze to figure out what the writer is saying; he just says it—and says it memorably. Who can forget Proverbs 15:1, which says, "A gentle answer turns away wrath, but a harsh word stirs up anger"? Or "As iron sharpens iron, so one person sharpens another" (Proverbs 27:17)? Short, sweet, and true as true can be.

In the same way, I think seasoned leaders ought to be able to pinpoint their guiding principles on the important stuff of leadership and distill them down to memorable sound-bites that can be called upon at a second's notice to inform a critical decision.

For more than three decades I've had the privilege of leading Willow Creek Community Church. And for the better part of that tenure, I've led by axioms—leadership proverbs that I have created and practiced, albeit mostly only by "oral tradition." Recently I decided it was time to craft them in written form, which explains how this book came to fruition. I joked with my publisher that this book took me three decades to write and three months to get on paper! While I have put some structure to these axioms, feel free to dive in anywhere and stay as long as you like. When you land on a concept that's especially helpful to you, use the "Links" section at its conclusion to be steered toward other similarly themed axioms. Each chapter requires less than a ten-minute commitment on your part but will hopefully help you for a lifetime.

oduction

vision & strategy

1 | LANGUAGE MATTERS

If someone had tried to tell me thirty-five years ago that my effectiveness as a leader would often hinge on something as "inconsequential" as word choice, I'd have rolled my eyes and written them off. "As long as I can convey an idea in general terms that everyone can understand," I would have said, "I'll do just fine."

And I would have been dead wrong.

The truth is, leaders rise and fall by the language they use. Sometimes whole visions live or die on the basis of the words the leader chooses for articulating that vision.

The very best leaders I know wrestle with words until they are able to communicate their big ideas in a way that captures the imagination, catalyzes action, and lifts spirits. They coin creeds and fashion slogans and create rallying cries, all because they understand that language matters.

When you put the right words to a vision or a principle, it becomes axiomatic. It begins to live! It becomes memorable and powerful. It becomes *weight bearing*, and eventually everyone around you champions it. They defend it with vigor. They give to it and pray for it. Around Willow Creek Community Church I can say "Hire tens" to a senior leader or talk about "the umbrella of mercy" with volunteers or rave that a recent event was an "only God" moment to a member of the congregation, and they get what I'm saying immediately. It's like speaking in shorthand—"insider" language that deepens community and creates clarity and a special sort of solidarity.

The very best leaders I know wrestle with words until they are able to communicate their big ideas in a way that captures the imagination, catalyzes action, and lifts spirits. They coin creeds and fashion slogans and create rallying cries, all because they understand that language matters. Axioms bolster a culture and steady it against the winds of change. Choose the right words and you'll set up everyone you lead for a level of effectiveness you never thought could be achieved.

Strange though it may seem, I often take long walks around our campus in search of one key word for a leadership talk I'm working on. One word. I've been known to devote an entire transatlantic flight to nailing a *single sentence* for an important vision talk that I need to give to Willow. Sound psychotic to you? The point I'm making is that words really do matter. And leaders must pay the price to choose the right ones, because when they do, the payoff is huge.

Willow just went through a massive strategic planning process. It took us a year and a half to do it, but I know the benefits will far surpass whatever time and energy we devoted to getting it right. Our ministry leaders and senior staff met repeatedly to talk about what was firing them up and what they believed God wanted our church to look like in coming years. The conversation kept coming back to three key values: evangelism, discipleship, and compassion.

With that solved, many of our leaders were relieved. *Finally!* they thought. *We know exactly what God wants us to focus on!* But those of us with a few decades of leadership under our belts knew that our work had only begun. We knew that if we wanted to raise congregational enthusiasm for our strategic plan, we were going to have to search for words that would grab the hearts and minds of our people and move them to action.

It was a task that proved every bit as difficult as discerning the key values in the first place. But after dozens of iterations, we landed on the right words. For example, we didn't want to talk merely about evangelism; instead, we said that we wanted to "raise the level of risk" in our attempt to point people to faith in Christ. Willow has always been a risk-taking church, a character-istic that motivates the entrepreneurial spirit so pervasive in our congrega-tion. To think that after thirty-three years, our church would be riskier than it had ever been got people amped up fast. Thankfully, our "raise the risk" description instantly elicited people's very best energy, something we'd des-perately need if we hoped to mobilize our entire congregation toward higher levels of evangelistic engagement.

Next up was discipleship, but we didn't want to talk merely about disci-pleship. Instead, we chose to do something we'd never done in the history of our church. We built an apology right into the verbiage of our strategic plan. We said to our congregation, "As it relates to discipleship, in the next three years, we're going to *rethink* how we coach people toward full devotion to Christ." It was a confession of sorts. We were admitting that we should have been doing better at challenging Christ-followers toward full devotedness, and so we promised we'd marshal the best ideas and tools and resources and make improvements going forward. "Rethinking" implied both honesty about our effectiveness or lack thereof, in the past, and intentionality regarding the future. We were going to turn over every stone to help move believers boldly toward complete maturity in Christ. And the congregation loved it.

Then came compassion. But instead of just saying we were going to "be compassionate," (big yawn), we said we were going to "unleash unprecedented amounts of compassion into our broken world." When people heard that phrase during Vision Weekend, they applauded for sixty seconds straight. We had struck a deep chord with the congregation, mainly because of the careful selection of just two words, "unleash" and "unprecedented."

Raise the risk. Rethink. Unleash. Even the cadence of the terms was important to our leadership team as we thought through what language to use. At the risk of piling on, let me say it again: language matters!

I try to apply the same rigorous approach to message titling as well. One time I worked with a concept for six months before I was finally able to label it.

I kept explaining to people a sense of "spiritual angst" I was feeling over things like extreme poverty and the HIV/AIDS pandemic and patterns of racism that still exist in this country and around the world. Listeners didn't latch onto that term, so I tried another: "It's like a sense of *divine frustration*." Blank stares came back at me. Something was obviously amiss. Those two words just didn't connect with people. *Spiritual angst* and *divine frustration* didn't arrest people in the same way the actual concept was arresting me. I kept at it and kept at it until finally, I landed on the phrase *holy discontent*.[1] Once that label showed up, people went nuts. Finally, they could relate. Instinctively, they knew what it meant. And instantly, they wanted to know more. I was asked to give that talk all over the world, and it eventually became a book. Ah, the beautiful by-product of choosing the right words.

In one-on-one conversations, I exercise this same discipline. If I need to have a significant conversation with a colleague, I write down my thoughts in a journal before I ever step foot into the meeting room. The other person is probably going to remember only a few sentences from our conversation, so I want to work hard to select accurate phrases of note.

For instance, if a serious problem exists with an underperforming staff member—especially if that person has been confronted by others before my meeting with them—I might look at them and say, "This is your 911 call. What we're dealing with right here, right now, carries with it the top level of urgency and importance. If this behavior does not change—*immediately*—you'll be asked to leave our staff. This is what I want you to remember when you walk out of the room today. Nine-one-one ... are we clear?"

We usually are.

In other situations in which the other person may *believe* the stakes are high when in fact they are not, I will relieve them early in the conversation by saying, "This subject is important, but please understand me: we are not in an emergency here. There are no blinking red lights, no wailing sirens, and no secret agents cleaning out your office while you're in here. Are you with me?

"What I *am* saying," I continue, "is that over a reasonable period of time your manager and I need to see dramatic improvement in this area. The only thing I'm after today is your strong commitment to improvement. Deal?"

Language matters! The right words will make vision talks soar. Carefully chosen phrases can make strategic plans sound like rally cries. Do the work, and you'll experience the payoff.

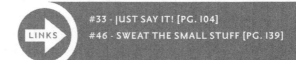

LINKS

#33 - JUST SAY IT! [PG. 104]
#46 - SWEAT THE SMALL STUFF [PG. 139]

2 | MAKE THE BIG ASK

Leadership is a lot about asking. After casting bold visions, leaders ask people to help make them become reality. Leaders describe pressing problems that are imperiling mission achievement and then ask people to devote their best thinking and most innovative ideas to solve them. In church work, leaders ask spiritual seekers to consider Christ. They ask believers to grow up in their faith. They ask staff members and volunteers and donors and contractors to show up and give their best time and money and energy and heart—all because they believe so much in the cause they're pursuing.

So I realized long ago that "asking" would always be a significant part of my leadership role. What I *didn't* know was that the longer I led, the bigger my "asks" would get. I had no choice: God was laying big visions on my mind and heart, and the only way they were going to get translated into reality was if some big asks were made.

One of the biggest challenges I have ever led involved an expansion effort we did at Willow. As far as I knew, it would require the largest capital campaign ever attempted by a local church. The stakes felt sky-high, and I frequently had to remind myself that I was going to have to be absolutely shameless in asking people to join me in this grand, God-glorifying endeavor.

And shamelessly ask I did ... publicly, privately, and prayerfully.

In the end God worked powerfully, resulting in the launch of several dynamic regional campuses, a terrific new facility at our Barrington location, and increased funding for the WCA (Willow Creek Association). But it also yielded an interesting insight: when handled properly, people are actually quite flattered to be asked to do significant things for God. Granted, they might not always say yes—they *can't* always say yes—but they are almost always honored by a wise and well-timed ask.

> *I realized long ago that "asking" would always be a significant part of my leadership role. What I didn't know was that the longer I led, the bigger my "asks" would get.*

I saw this even more clearly once I found myself on the receiving end of a few big asks. I'd been leading Willow for a couple of decades when authors started asking for book endorsements, organizations started asking me to serve on their boards, and charities started asking for large financial gifts to help their ministries. Interestingly, each time one of these big asks came in, I'd realize I wasn't offended in the least. In fact, I felt quite honored.

When someone asked me to help advance their cause, I'd think, "Wow. They must think I'm kingdom-oriented enough to care about something like this. What's more, they must think I actually have a contribution to make in achieving their goal."

When they'd ask for money, I'd think, "They assume I've handled whatever financial resources have come my way responsibly enough that I would have the capacity to do this." What a compliment!

I've become a huge advocate of leaders getting clear in their heads about both the necessity of big asks and the way to make them wisely, because when they're done well, they can actually build relationships. When they're done well, there is rarely a downside.

Let me offer a simple framework that I keep handy so that whenever God prompts me to make a big ask, I'm ready. First, it's important to set the context. Often over a lunch table, I'll say, "God has led me to challenge you with something today, but please know from the outset that we'll be okay whether you accept this challenge or not. My goal here is to be obedient to God's prompting, not to force you to do something. I have zero attachment to the course of action you choose on the back end of our discussion today. It won't affect our friendship or my respect for you because this is not between you and me as much as it is between you and God. Are we on the same page here?"

Second, when I make the ask, I do it as clearly and succinctly as possible. On many occasions, I have sat across the dinner table from a seeker and said, "Tonight's the night I'm going to ask you to receive Christ. You may not be ready, and that will be fine, but I want to briefly review how God's love can change a human heart and then give you an opportunity to respond."

I've sat across from marketplace people and said, "In a few minutes, I'm going to ask you to consider joining our ministry staff. Before I do that, though, I want to give you four reasons why I am challenging you to join our ministry team. When I am done, I really want you to pray about leaving your job and coming on board with our staff."

I've sat across from high-capacity executives and said, "I'm asking you to consider volunteering your time to our board." I've sat across from billionaires and said, "I'd like to ask you to pray about giving more of your hard-earned money to God's purposes in the world."

Sure, sometimes I feel a bit nervous and have a lump in my throat during conversations like these, but there's just no escaping the fact that effective leadership requires growing in this skill. And I know the more confidently I do it, the better off everyone will be.

After making the ask, I always suggest that the other person take it before God and then get back to me in an agreed-upon amount of time. "Could we meet again in a week [or two, or four] to see where you are with this?" I ask. Sometimes that subsequent meeting yields a no. But just as frequently I've had people return to me with a "Hey, I'm in! I brought your request to God, and he gave me a green light!"

Again, when the making of the ask is handled in a spiritually and relationally intelligent manner, there is very seldom a downside. Any outcome is fine.

The nature of human beings is such that we tend not to *drift* into better behaviors. We usually have to be *asked* by someone to consider taking it up a level.

In my own life, I've rarely made a sizable step forward—spiritually, physically, emotionally, or otherwise—unless someone asked me to do so. Along the way, I've radically altered my eating and exercise habits because exceptional leaders have asked me to consider becoming a healthier person. I've channeled resources toward worthy causes because courageous leaders have asked me to help them achieve a compelling vision. I've parented more intentionally, supported my wife with greater devotion, practiced spiritual disciplines more faithfully, and upped the ante on my own leadership development, to name just a few, all because gutsy leaders asked me to do so.

And each time, I'd think, "Maybe I really can take it up a notch. I'd just never thought much about it until now."

If you're chasing a bold vision, one of the greatest gifts you can give the people around you is to get in front of them, eyeball-to-eyeball, and ask them to step up and do something great for God. Do it well, and you'll bring glory to God, esteem to the other person, and much-needed resources to your ministry.

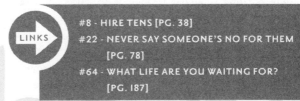

LINKS

#8 - HIRE TENS [PG. 38]
#22 - NEVER SAY SOMEONE'S NO FOR THEM
     [PG. 78]
#64 - WHAT LIFE ARE YOU WAITING FOR?
     [PG. 187]

vision and strategy | 23

3 | You're Always in a Season

All sorts of studies are being done these days to tout the importance of self-awareness in the life of a leader. I couldn't agree more: at any given moment, you've got to be able to step back and assess how you're doing as a leader and where you're going, what's working well and what is not. But I have always believed in the importance of doing the same kind of thing with regard to the organizations I lead.

I'm in and out of local churches nearly every week, and I love to test leaders' organizational awareness by asking a straightforward question: "What season are you in as a church?" The most perceptive leaders I know fire back an answer to that question without batting an eye: "We're in a growth season right now," or "We've been on a plateau for far too long, and people are getting frustrated," or "We've run our volunteers ragged and probably need to slow the pace and let people catch their breath," or "We've gone through more change cycles in the past ninety days than should be legal, but things are finally starting to settle out a bit."

A key responsibility of the leader is to know what season the organization is in, to name it, and then to communicate the implications of that season to his or her followers.

An easy season to identify is a *season of growth*. In a growth season, everything is rosy. Attendance is spiking, giving is on the rise, programs are thriving, and the future looks bright. In seasons like this, leaders have to be organizationally aware enough to say, "Look, everybody, we're going through a fun growth spurt here. Let's pour *all* of our energies into fueling the fires of growth. Let's enjoy this season and play it out for as long as we can. You know as well as I do that it won't last forever, but while it's here, let's thank God for it and see how long we can keep it going!"

Another season might be called *consolidation*, which usually follows a season of growth.

The goal during consolidations is to assimilate and support the people who showed up during all of that growth. Newcomers typically need discipleship and community and care. Investing in your infrastructure and protecting your recent gains proves you can be trusted with the growth God graciously gives. Effective consolidation earns you permission to enter yet another season of growth sometime in your future.

Another season that is familiar to leaders is a season of *transition*. It might begin when several staff decide to leave all at once, and everything and everyone feels a bit off balance and uncertain. It might be complicated by external factors such as a downturn in the local economy or a major upheaval in the community, and leaders are the ones who must give voice and language to that reality. They must explain why the era is occurring, what it means, and how to navigate through it.

> *A key responsibility of the leader is to know what season the organization is in, to name it, and then to communicate the implication of that season to his or her followers.*

A season most leaders dread is *malaise*. In this season, things are unusually somber, stale, and just plain stuck. Everything feels dated, and there is no buzz to be found. "We need to shake up this organization," the leader might say, "because failing to do so might make the malaise permanent. And who wants that?"

Finally, there's *reinvention*. This is when the leader announces that it's time to put every ministry of the church under the microscope and discern whether it needs a face-lift, an overhaul, or a funeral—a necessary pruning exercise to make room for future growth.

This leadership-seasons idea traces back to Ecclesiastes 3:1, which says that "there is a time for everything, and a season for every activity under the heavens." Most leaders nod consent at that line of thinking but simultaneously neglect to tell their followers what season they're in! And based on my experience, people sitting in your organization will have no clue what season they're in unless you tell them.

Do yourself and those you lead the favor of learning to spot the changing of the seasons in your environment. When you see growth bloom or transition hit or feel the icy days of malaise descend, draw attention to the shift. Give voice to the realities of that season. Assign appropriate language to it, designate helpful parameters to succeeding within it, and confidently offer solutions for moving through it. You're always in a season, leader. It's your role to know which it is and what to do about it.

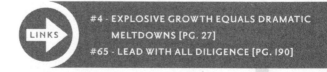

#4 - EXPLOSIVE GROWTH EQUALS DRAMATIC MELTDOWNS [PG. 27]
#65 - LEAD WITH ALL DILIGENCE [PG. 190]

4 | EXPLOSIVE GROWTH EQUALS DRAMATIC MELTDOWNS

Most people are not aware of the fact that in certain places around the world, the local church is experiencing phenomenal growth — growth that sounds eerily like the kind described in Acts 2:47, which says that the Lord "added to their number daily those who were being saved."

Occasionally I will have dinner with a pastor of one of these fast-growing churches and hear words like these: "Bill, we've just been through an *explosive* season of growth. We did an outreach event and grew by 50 percent in thirty days and are just in awe of what is happening!"

Knowing this dynamic all too well, I typically look back at the overjoyed pastor and say something like, "Way to go! I'm so pleased that you're making advances for the kingdom! Really, I thank God with you! Can I just ask you one question? Are your internal structures and systems capable of supporting all of that growth?"

The blank stare in response usually answers my question.

No matter what type of church you serve and on what continent you serve it, the temptation for all church leaders being blessed by God-given growth is to delight themselves fully in the influx of new people but then forget to plan for how to actually *assimilate* those people into their ministry. They add a few hundred folks in a brief burst of time and then realize all of a sudden that they are out of parking

> *No matter what type of church you serve and on what continent you serve it, the temptation for all church leaders being blessed by God-given growth is to delight themselves fully in the influx of new people but then forget to plan for how to actually assimilate those people into their ministry.*

space, they are short fifty children's workers, and by putting folding chairs in the aisles they are in violation of several different fire codes.

One time at Willow, we orchestrated a massive evangelistic plan within our congregation. During the final few weeks leading up to that event, we gathered as a leadership team and begged God to anoint our effort. Graciously, he did just that. In spades.

We were inundated by new people who came to check out the church, and to our horror, we didn't have enough parking spaces to accommodate them. There were hundreds of cars stacked four-deep along our campus's roads—both inbound *and* outbound. Nicely dressed adults trudged through fields of grass and mud to reach the front door. Children were thrust into already-overcrowded classrooms and asked to sit quietly in a stuffy space for a full ninety minutes. Talk about a systemic meltdown of dramatic proportions! To say we were embarrassed would be an understatement. It was awful. God had done his part. We just hadn't done ours.

Our excitement over all that new growth was quickly tempered by the painful reality that we had dropped the ball. We had dropped a *dozen* balls. We had been so singularly focused on our plans to get new people into our church that we failed to provide necessary infrastructure in the event that all that planning actually bore fruit.

My hard-won advice? Have a bold plan for explosive growth! Expect God to answer your fervent prayers and to do his part in bringing people your way. Just be sure to tend to the needs that all that growth will bring. And at the very same time, roll up your sleeves and figure out how you are going to assimilate those new folks so that someday, every one of them will become fully yielded to Christ and fully integrated into your church.

LINKS

#3 - YOU'RE ALWAYS IN A SEASON [PG. 24]
#15 - THE DANGERS OF INCREMENTALISM [PG. 56]
#46 - SWEAT THE SMALL STUFF [PG. 139]

5 | VISION: PAINT THE PICTURE PASSIONATELY

In 1774 a leader named John Adams boldly declared, "Someday, I see a union of thirteen states, a new nation, independent from the Parliament and the King of England." He was the first to express that idea publicly. And just a few years later, against all odds, the United States of America was born.

Fifteen years later, an Englishman named William Wilberforce stood before the British Parliament and lobbied for the day when slaves would no longer be bought and sold like farm animals. It took decades to get it done, but eventually the slave trade was officially abolished all across the United Kingdom.

In the late 1800s, the Wright brothers pictured a day when people would soar through the sky aboard a metal capsule with wings. Ten years later, on December 17, 1903, the Wright Flyer made its first ascent from the sandy beach in North Carolina.

In the 1940s, Billy Graham and a few college buddies gathered together and dreamed of filling stadiums all over the world, presenting the gospel to people who were far from God. As of this writing, through the efforts they've led, 215 million[2] have heard the gospel message in person, and well over a billion have heard it via television and radio.

More personally, in 1973, Dr. Gilbert Bilezikian stood behind a college classroom lectern and shared his dream for building a prevailing church — a biblically functioning, Acts 2 community of faith that would be relevant to this age. He spoke of a church that would reach lost people with the gospel, then assimilate those people into the body of Christ and equip and empower them for service. He dreamed of a church that would help care for the poor, invite them into community with one another, and glorify God in everything.

The one thing common to all these leaders is this: they all had *vision*.

At the core of leadership sits the power of vision, in my estimation the most potent offensive weapon in the leader's arsenal. It has been defined dozens of ways, but for me, the crispest articulation of vision is that it's a "picture of the future that produces passion in people."

A brand-new country, young and free. The shackles of slavery broken once and for all. People flying across a clear blue sky. Thousands of women, men, and children rising to their feet and flooding the altar at the first strains of "Just as I Am." Acts 2 churches invading the modern world. Whatever the picture, if it produces powerful amounts of passion in those who hear it, it is already en route to being achieved.

For you it might be the picture of a hungry child being fed, her life being spared. It might be a picture of a homeless person finding shelter. It might be a picture of a dying church being revitalized or a lost person coming to faith or a volunteer finding a ministry that perfectly uses the gifts God has given. It might be a lonely person finding community or an artist finally using his creative gifts to serve God. There are as many life-giving, visionary pictures of the future as there are leaders among us. And when God finally brings clarity and certainty of vision in a leader's life, *everything* changes for the better.

There are as many life-giving, visionary pictures of the future as there are leaders among us. And when God finally brings clarity and certainty of vision in a leader's life, everything changes for the better.

When I first heard Dr. B at Trinity College casting the vision of life in a biblically functioning Christian community, emotions welled up inside of me that I'd never known. Sometimes while he was talking about the potential of a local church, I felt the passion so strongly I could barely keep myself from crying. Other times I wanted to jump up and shout, "Gang, this is it! Don't you see it? Can't you feel it? The local church is the hope of the world! It's the God-ordained redemptive agency that the future of the entire world hangs on. Cancel your career plans! Do something important with your one and only life! Lay it down for the sake of the local church!"

That was thirty-plus years ago, and I still remember those feelings as vividly as if it were today. In fact, if you strapped a heart monitor to my chest today while someone talks about the beauty or the wonder or the potential of the local church, it would beep and smoke and flash, "Danger, danger, danger!"

The local church — it still stirs the deepest kinds of feelings in me. Nothing else does this to me. I've had some other exhilarating experiences in my life, but they pale in comparison to what stirs in my heart when it comes to giving my life to help renew the local church. Vision and passion are inextricably bound together in the life of a leader. God made it so. When you have eyes to see the vision that God has given to you, you'll know it because your heart will feel it so deeply that, over time, any lingering uncertainty will vanish.

Leaders, don't ever apologize for the strength of feeling you have for the vision that God has put into your life. Don't hide your feelings about it. God meant for you to feel as deeply about his vision for you as you do about anything. I mean that! *Anything.* Paint your God-given vision for family, friends, colleagues, and total strangers, if they will listen. Paint it as colorfully and passionately as you can! Just get it painted so that people's hearts are stirred enough to shout, "Count me in!"

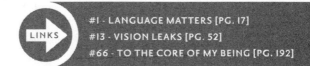

LINKS

#1 - LANGUAGE MATTERS [PG. 17]
#13 - VISION LEAKS [PG. 52]
#66 - TO THE CORE OF MY BEING [PG. 192]

6 | BOLD MOVE

Back in the days when neither seatbelts nor infant car seats were mandatory, my daughter, Shauna, would sit right by my side on the arm rest of the old Chevy Impala I drove.

One morning she and I loaded up to run a few errands, and as I was pulling out onto a major thoroughfare, I glanced over to make sure she was secure on her makeshift seat. In that split second between when I looked her way and when I looked back to see any oncoming traffic, a car appeared out of nowhere. Feeling I had no other options, I stomped on the accelerator. The other driver came within mere feet of plowing into us before swerving out of our lane. It was way too close for comfort, and I died a thousand deaths in the space of the next six shallow breaths. What if that car had hit us? What if Shauna had been hurt? Or killed?

My mind was racing as I tried to think of a way to apologize to this little girl who because of me almost didn't make it to her fifth birthday, when she interrupted my self-reproach with three simple words: "Bold move, Dad."

It wasn't the first time Shauna had leveled me with her wit. At four, she could verbalize things better than people far older. I was so struck by the humor of her comment that as soon as we got home, I told Lynne the whole story. I told my close friends. One time I even told the congregation at Willow during a weekend service. And eventually, the phrase stuck.

These days, we use it to describe courageous, high-risk plans that God just might use in a major way. Recently I heard a Creeker (my term of endearment for a participating member of Willow Creek) telling one of my colleagues that he was trying to get all twenty of his senior executives to come with him to our annual Leadership Summit. My wide-eyed colleague said simply, "Bold move!"

Once you label something in a culture, you give it an identity. You legitimize it and, in so doing, increase the likelihood that you'll see that behavior on an ever-increasing basis. Why? Because people become organizational heroes when they exhibit it!

As the years went by, my teammates and I began to notice that the primary reason we were making significant progress as a church was that we had enough people making "bold moves." They were thinking fresh thoughts, pioneering cool new programs, and trusting God to accomplish significant kingdom-building activity in their midst.

What has been true for us is true for you too: you will never take big hills without making bold moves. The alternative is incrementalism, which is dangerous and often deadly to organizations. Incrementalism says, "Hey, let's increase the effectiveness of our current efforts by 2 percent a year but then expect a *huge* increase in effectiveness to occur sometime in the future!" That seldom works.

> *What has been true for us is true for you too: you will never take big hills without making bold moves.*

Incrementalism and innovation make terrible bedfellows. Make a few bold moves, or you'll breathe your last leadership breath far too soon.

Your move.

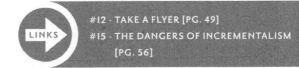

LINKS

#12 - TAKE A FLYER [PG. 49]
#15 - THE DANGERS OF INCREMENTALISM [PG. 56]

7 | An Owner or a Hireling

Acts 20 and 21 record the story of the apostle Paul's emotional farewell to some fellow leaders as he was about ready to board a ship and sail off to his next assignment. The church he had started with a handful of friends had grown like a weed, and Paul was having the time of his life, but now God had a new thing for him to do. The Spirit was compelling him: "Paul, I want you to spread my word in Jerusalem just as you've done in Ephesus."

As exciting as a brand-new calling from heaven might sound, Paul knew that this one was going to be complicated by the fact that Christians in Jerusalem were being arrested, flogged, and killed. The risk was ridiculously high, but Paul had clearly heard from God. And so, in response to this new vision he was being asked to pursue, he offered up a powerful three-letter word: *Yes.*

He resigned from his church, packed his bags, and set sail for Jerusalem.

At one port along the way, Paul was intercepted by a prophet who obviously questioned Paul's judgment. "You have no idea what awaits you there, Paul! If you insist on taking this trip, it very likely will cost you your life."

"But it's a vision from God," Paul replied. "I *have* to carry it out."

The prophet was flabbergasted. In one of the strangest accounts in the New Testament, he untied Paul's belt and proceeded to lie down on the ground and bind his own hands and feet like a calf at the county rodeo. If Paul refused to listen to the prophet's words, then maybe a visual would clear things up. "You just don't get it, do you! Look at me! You set one foot in the Jerusalem city limits, Paul, and you'll be bound, beaten, and killed!"

To which Paul said, "I think *you're* the one who doesn't get it! The God of heaven and earth has entrusted a vision to me. I am ready not only to be bound and beaten, but to die in Jerusalem for the name of the Lord Jesus Christ, should it come to that!"[3]

The text says that when the prophet discerned that Paul could not be dissuaded, he said, "Then God's will be done."[4]

The passage wrecks me every single time I read it. It wrecked me again just now. Leaders have to contend with this idea of how seriously we will pursue our God-given visions. It's a one-on-one conversation between God and the leader alone, but the implications of that dialogue are huge. Wise leaders understand that the single greatest determinant of whether followers will ever own a vision deeply is the extent to which those followers believe the *leader* will own it.

I've learned the hard way that you can't fool people on this one. They see and smell and sense just how deep your ownership goes. They know whether you're an owner or an hourly worker—a "hired hand," as Jesus called halfhearted people who labored in the sheep-protection business of his day. You know the type: they're committed to the vision God gave them to carry out until it gets too hard, the price gets too high, the fun factor gets overshadowed by onerous challenges, and the honeymoon gets declared over and done.

Wise leaders understand that the single greatest determinant of whether followers will ever own a vision deeply is the extent to which those followers believe the leader will own it.

Based on empirical evidence, your followers will formulate an assessment of the depth of your ownership and will adjust their ownership accordingly. Your followers take their cues from you. They will only sacrifice for the vision if you will. They will only take a bullet for the cause if they believe down to their toes that you would do the same. Are you a halfhearted, low-cost hireling? Or are you a full-on owner? Your followers are immensely curious about which it is, and over time each of them will come to a conclusion.

A couple of months ago, I was at the end of a strenuous international trip. I was standing in the customs-and-immigration line at the Johannesburg airport with the top two people from the Willow Creek Association International. We were headed to South America, which was a mere four-movie flight from where we stood. But it would be our final stop on this three-week trip before heading home. I was tired, but I felt I had one more country in me.

My colleagues got through customs and immigration without a hitch, and then it was my turn. I had been handed a new passport just before leaving the States because my old one had filled up, and apparently someone back home had forgotten to insert my Brazilian visa for this trip. "I'm sorry,

Mr. Hybels," the South African clerk said, "but you cannot go to Brazil without that visa."

My frustration was eclipsed by the realization that this oversight obviously meant I would get to go home a few days ahead of schedule. *Nice!*

Or maybe not.

Gary Schwammlein, the WCA's international director, looked at the clerk and asked how we could get the visa situation resolved. "Bill *must* be at our Brazil meetings," he explained, as if this would overturn governmental policy.

"There's only one way he can get there," the clerk said. "Mr. Hybels can fly to Dakar, Senegal" (a very long flight away and not exactly a resort destination), "and then from there fly to Washington, D.C., to obtain a travel visa from the Brazilian embassy, and then from there fly to his final destination in South America."

"Well, that solves *that*," I said reflexively. I just knew that no one would expect me to go through all of that for one final stop.

Or *maybe* no one.

Gary looked at his colleague and then at me and said, "You know, Bill, we're not asking you to take a beating or to shed blood. . . ."

He let that clarification linger in the air before he smiled and continued, "We're just asking you to watch a *whole* bunch of movies."

I didn't smile back.

I went to the hotel and wrestled with God for several hours. "Hey, *I* didn't make the mistake here. Other people handle my passport, and they screwed this up — not me!"

God was unfazed.

At the end of my bulletproof rationale, all I heard was a still, small voice saying, "I've given you an entrustment, Bill, and it includes Brazil. Christians before you have been willing to pay a far higher price than to ride modern airliners and watch movies for an extra twenty thousand miles. Just go."

So I did. I flew to Dakar and I flew to D.C., where I stood in long lines for many hours to obtain a new visa, and I flew all night down to Brazil. Upon landing, I had a meeting with a group of pastors that I will remember for the rest of my life.

When I was finally headed back to Chicago, I couldn't help but think what a huge loss it would have been if I had missed that powerful time of mutual encouragement in South America with men and women who are gracefully, passionately fighting the good fight for the kingdom every single day of their lives. What an inspiration!

At some point in their leadership journey, every leader gets a vision from God. They start to carry out that vision and feel extremely privileged to be doing God's bidding here on earth. But then the road forks. One path leads to *hireling* status, the other to that of *owner*. I watch leaders come to this intersection all the time and make their choice. Some head down the hireling path, and it wreaks havoc for everyone. The vision becomes more about them, their career, their fame, their success. Discerning people around them say, "What happened to you? You were never like this before!" And one by one, key followers bail out. They have to; the deal has changed.

The compromised leader might well continue to lead, but eventually everyone figures out that God will never fully bless the efforts of this hireling. When that time comes, it's game, set, match.

Other leaders come to that critical intersection and instead choose the *owner* path. They say, "God, you gave me this vision, and it's your power that's fueling it and your people who are accomplishing it and your glory alone that we're all fighting for. Right here and right now, I tell you all over again that I will pay any price to achieve this vision so that someday, when I get to the finish line, I'll be able to say with Paul that I fought the good fight."

These leaders wake up every day ready to do battle on behalf of their God-given visions for one simple reason: their commendation is coming. "Well done," Christ promises to say to them. "Well done. You did it as an owner, all the way to the end." Take the owner path, my friend. Your followers will notice and will be inspired to do great things for God's glory.

LINKS

#29 - SPEED OF THE LEADER, SPEED OF THE TEAM [PG. 94]
#54 - EVERY SOLDIER DESERVES COMPETENT COMMAND [PG. 161]

vision and strategy | 37

8 | HIRE TENS

As much as I hate using a numeric scale to describe the effectiveness of a leader, occasionally it does serve a purpose. Let's say I have a staff leader who is about a five on the leadership-effectiveness scale, ten being the highest. He or she works hard but does not take responsibility to get better as a leader and does not seek out a coach or a mentor. The five rating appears to be a long-term fixture.

As unfortunate as this is, what complicates matters is that a five can never attract, motivate, or retain people who are *higher* on the effectiveness scale than they are. Fives can recruit and mobilize and retain fours and threes and twos and ones, but no matter how hard they try, fives cannot lead sixes or eights or tens. Likewise, eights can lead and empower sevens and sixes, but give them a nine and the nine will soon bail. Leadership just works like that.

One day it dawned on me that my objective as a senior leader needed to be not only taking responsibility to increase my own level of effectiveness so that I stood firmly in the eight, nine, or ten range, but also surrounding myself with people who were as close to my level as possible. Because collectively, while we would be able to attract people who were *equal to or lower than* we were on the leadership-effectiveness scale, we'd never recruit and retain those above us. Still today I constantly challenge my team to do their very best to raise their level through participating in leadership development and training and reading all they can read.

But I also challenge them never to shrink back from inviting leaders at their same level to come join our cause. Only the most mature leaders can overcome the great temptation to enlist the first warm, willing, low-numbered body they see. After all, people who rank lower on the scale are typically more malleable, less stressful to manage, and more easily impressed by a leader's prowess. They make for a spectacular ego stroke. It's a stroke that comes at a high price, though, because when it's time for that person to invite someone onto the team, they'll follow suit and look for people with scary-low leadership levels.

Over time, the net effect of hiring people less effective than you is an ever-increasing number of lower-caliber leaders. Eventually this compromises the quality of leadership in the entire organization.

Train and embolden your staff members to grow their own leadership and then to shoot high when someone needs to be added to the team. Encourage them to go after the brightest, most accomplished, most effective leaders they can find. In so doing, you will continually upgrade your organization's leadership capabilities.

Embolden your staff members to grow their own leadership and then to shoot high when someone needs to be added to the team. Encourage them to go after the brightest, most accomplished, most effective leaders they can find. In so doing, you will continually upgrade your organization's leadership capabilities.

I've been in various church services when pastors have poked fun at the disciples Jesus chose, as if the Messiah shot low and went after misfits. I don't think this is the case at all. True, he didn't necessarily surround himself with aristocrats. But a careful profile analysis reveals that guys like James and Peter and Paul—a *monster* leader to whom Jesus made a special appearance on the Damascus Road—had quite high leadership capabilities. And when his action-oriented, high-capacity direct reports were thrown the kingdom ball, they scored in a way that would count for all of history.

May the same be said of us. With every recruit we invite into the game, let's be found guilty of gradually *upgrading* the leadership talent of the local church so that our contribution can count for all of history too.

LINKS

#7 - AN OWNER OR A HIRELING [PG. 34]
#29 - SPEED OF THE LEADER, SPEED OF THE TEAM [PG. 94]
#54 - EVERY SOLDIER DESERVES COMPETENT COMMAND [PG. 161]
#65 - LEAD WITH ALL DILIGENCE [PG. 190]
#68 - READ ALL YOU CAN [PG. 196]
#73 - EXCELLENCE HONORS GOD AND INSPIRES PEOPLE [PG. 206]

9 | THE FAIR EXCHANGE VALUE

The fair exchange value comes right out of 1 Timothy 5, which says, "workers deserve their wages," or are worthy of their due.[5] In the vast majority of organizations, be they for-profit, not-for-profit, or public-sector, leaders try to extract the *most* output from staffers in exchange for the *least* amount of input—salary dollars, benefit perks, leadership development opportunities, vacation time, and so forth. Leaders often want maximum results, maximum effort, and maximum hours, regardless what a "fair exchange" would warrant.

I'm sad to say that Christian organizations have often fallen prey to this mindset as well. Some are simply being exploitive, while others are under-capitalized and struggle to attain the fair exchange value at all.

In the late 1970s and early 1980s, Willow staff members, under my guidance, were paid about a third of what they should have been making. We were millions of dollars in debt because of land purchases and building programs, and although we were doing our level best to spread our limited resources around fairly, the bitter truth remained: when it came to staff salaries, the exchange was *far* from fair.

After about year five of this, the staff-satisfaction level started to drop. One day, one of my best employees came into my office and said he was going to have to leave the staff and accept a position in the marketplace. I was stunned. "I'm having a ball," he explained. "I love this church, I love the vision, and I love your leadership. It's just that I have a family to raise, I'm the only breadwinner, and if my wife and I want to stay in this neighborhood and raise and educate our kids in this community, I'm going to have to find something that's a little more ... fair."

It was that word *fair* that nailed me. I had espoused the value of fairness for as long as I could remember, and here I was losing one of our best workers for one simple reason: I was violating the fair exchange value.

What I began to realize that day is that those staff members who joy-fully worked at Willow in the early days for a third of what they were worth secretly expected that at some point in the future, the situation would change. They never thought the sacrifices they signed up for would last a lifetime. You can imagine their surprise, then, when year after year they would see me launch more building programs and continue to hire people at low salaries, instead of using those resources to bring current salaries to appropriate levels.

I had espoused the value of fairness for as long as I could remember, and here I was losing one of my best workers for one simple reason: I was violating the fair exchange value.

Back to that meeting with the key staff member who said he was leaving the staff. Within seconds of his resignation, I asked, "If I were to find fair compensation for you, would you consider staying?"

He barely let me finish the question before he grabbed my hand to shake it and said, "No question about it. I'd work here the rest of my life if we could sort out this one issue."

Thirty-two years later, the guy is still on our staff.

LINKS

#60 - PAY NOW, PLAY LATER [PG. 174]
#67 - ALWAYS TAKE THE HIGH ROAD
[PG. 194]

10 | THE VALUE OF A GOOD IDEA

I was in Málaga, Spain, to train pastors several years back and because of flight schedules had some time to kill after the closing session. It was pouring down rain, which was fitting given the mood I was in. Back home, Willow was in a slump—a slump that bothered me every day, even across a very large ocean.

"I might be one good idea away from a message series that could fire up our church again," I thought. So I made a pact with God. "I'm going to walk up and down this beach until you give me a good idea. I believe you are a good God, and I am going to trust you to help me."

After I'd spent four hours trudging the soggy beach, it started to get dark. I'd toyed with a lot of ideas, but not a single *good* idea emerged. "I'm trusting you for this, God. One good idea. And I'm not beyond begging at this point!"

I made a U-turn at the end of the beach, shook the rain off the hood of my jacket, and started back for yet another lap when it hit me—not just a good idea, but a *really* good idea. "We should do an outreach-oriented sermon series. We could title it 'I Have a Friend Who ...' and we could invite the whole congregation to participate in creating the messages."

Regardless how it would get refined, one thing was certain: God had ponied up to my pact.

I ran back to my hotel room and wrote down as much of the idea as I could remember. Once back in the States, I shared it with my senior staff. They loved it and agreed that we should poll the congregation to see what needs their circles of friends had before we confirmed each week's theme. So we passed out index cards during a midweek service and asked every Creeker to think about their friends who weren't plugged into a church. "What keeps them from coming?" I asked from the stage. "What keeps them from trusting God with their lives? What are the major obstacles they face? Give us your best thoughts on these questions, and we'll give you the best messages and services we can come up with in response."

The top three vote-getters became the three talks for the series: "I Have a Friend Who Has Doubts about God," "I Have a Friend Who Struggles with Balancing Life's Demands," and "I Have a Friend Who Thinks All Religions Are the Same." We grew by a thousand people during those three weekends, most of whom are still with us today. What is the value of a good idea? A thousand lives added and tens of thousands of lives touched—all of which could be traced back to a desperate plea to God on a rainy day in Spain.

Looking back, I now see that whatever pockets of success Willow has known can *all* be traced back to a good idea. Because of a good idea, we launched a new kind of church in a movie theater in 1975. Because of a good idea, the Leadership Summit was born. Because of a good idea, the Global Summit emerged. Because of a good idea, sermon series were rolled out, ministries were launched, outreach events were held, and new staff structures were adopted.

Leaders traffic in idea creation. The best leaders I know are ferociously disciplined about seeking them out and incredibly committed to stewarding them well.

> *Leaders traffic in idea creation. The best leaders I know are ferociously disciplined about seeking them out and incredibly committed to stewarding them well.*

My good friend Bob Galvin was the brains and heart behind the Motorola Corporation's record-setting pace during the 1970s and 1980s. When he was at the operational helm of the company, he'd make senior leaders come to strategy meetings armed with a hundred good ideas about how to increase sales or improve R&D or generate greater market buzz. You couldn't get into the meeting unless you showed your list. Why? Because he knew what too few ministry leaders know: in order to land *one* good idea—one breakthrough idea that will kick your organization's activity into high gear—you have to allow for hundreds or even thousands of mediocre ideas. After all, if your big aha is number seventy-eight, you'll never discover it unless you discipline yourself and your team to think through numbers one through seventy-seven.

Along these lines, great leaders also know which people should be invited to idea-generation meetings in the first place. They know who will work hard and show up with long lists and who will not. And they try to make the meetings themselves a ball!

But there's more. Once a really good idea surfaces, you have to be a *fanatic* about stewarding it well. Great leaders keep a pad of paper and a pen by their bed so that ideas will be captured and not forgotten. When I'm on the road and a good idea hits, I often email my assistant, Jean, from my trusty BlackBerry. She'll get some cryptic message from Dubai or Singapore that says, "Please put these six words front and center on my desk for when I get back."

She has no idea what those six words mean, but she knows me well enough to know they're the genesis of a good idea. A good idea that might have huge impact.

Sometimes a good idea can simply spice up an otherwise bland event. Several years ago, Willow invited NFL coach and NASCAR team owner Joe Gibbs to come speak at our weekend services. Our programming team got together for a meeting to discuss the creative elements, the content of his talk, and the transitions. Everything seemed "fine"—the music scheduled was fine, the brief video of Gibbs's life that would precede his talk was fine, and we were quite sure the talk itself was going to be at least "fine." But something was missing.

"Gang, there's nothing 'really cool' about this service," I said. "There's not a single point in the service when people will scratch their heads in disbelief, thinking, 'How'd they come up with something as creative as that?'"

We had twenty minutes left in our allotted meeting time, so I said, "All right, bolt the doors. We've got to at least give this a shot. No idea is too stupid or too bizarre to be considered. Let's treat the sky as the limit for a few minutes and see what we come up with."

The first five or six ideas were, in fact, both stupid *and* bizarre, but then one of our drama guys spoke up. "What if we were to treat the transition between the video clip and Gibbs's talk like a pit stop? We could put a whole bunch of stagehands in NASCAR uniforms and have them do a dozen different chores super-fast as Joe takes the stage."

Smiles slowly appeared on faces. We were finally making progress.

We worked that idea through, sharpening it and adding elements to the original plan. The weekend arrived, the early part of the service went well, and just after we aired the video that told some of Joe's story, our mock pit crew sprang into action. One person dropped the lectern into position while another took a bottle of Windex to it, furiously cleaning it as if it were the windshield of a race car. In the space of thirteen seconds, things were rolled into position, straightened up, tightened down, and spit-shined. Once the flurry of activity ended, the uniformed volunteers jumped over a fake pit wall and dashed to their front-row seats as if nothing had happened.

It absolutely blew everyone's mind and in the end was the highlight of the entire service, even by Joe Gibbs's assessment. It was in fact a good idea! (And not mine.) But it did require pushing for it. You get the point.

LINKS

#27 - GET THE RIGHT PEOPLE AROUND THE
TABLE [PG. 91]
#43 - A BLUE-SKY DAY [PG. 131]
#73 - EXCELLENCE HONORS GOD AND
INSPIRES PEOPLE [PG. 206]

11 | BUILD A BOILER FUND

Sadly, some of the finest ministries the world has ever known have had to lay off their staffs, shut their doors, and sell their facilities. This unnerved me for many years. I wondered, "Is there a mysterious force at work in the world that is capable of wrecking even the best-led ministries?" Eventually I figured out that mismanagement was the cause of many organizational funerals. And to get even more specific, quite often a naive notion of "profit" played a particularly ruinous role.

Accordingly, I have come to believe that every ministry, *including* the local church, must be profitable. "But you can't possibly mean that!" horrified pastors burst out in response. I do. To some, it's a shocking posture to hold because they misinterpret it to read, "Let's rake in all the money we can and then divvy it up among the principals!"

But that couldn't be further from my intentions. The painful truth is that unless we become consistently profitable, we will not exist to minister another day.

I push this position on every senior church leader I coach, but it's never an easy sell. "But aren't we supposed to be *non*profit?" they ask. "Even *officially* so?"

> *The painful truth is that unless we become consistently profitable, we will not exist to minister another day.*

Yes, I explain, but *you* try hiding behind your nonprofit status when you stand before God someday and are asked to explain why your wonderful, divinely anointed ministry had to close its doors.

One of many damaging by-products of the nonprofit-and-proud-of-it mentality has been the creation and near-religious adherence to "balanced budgets." Christian organizations are notorious for propagating the idea that if, in a fiscal year, you take in $2.5 million, you must spend $2.5 million—a *full* $2.5 million. Achieve that and you get to throw a big party to celebrate. (I wonder who is paying for *that* party. Was it in the budget?)

At Willow, our "balanced budget" includes a significant contribution to reserves and substantial "set-asides" for operating contingency funds. Once all of that is included in our budget, we work hard and pray fervently that we will reach our revenue target and stay disciplined with spending.

All leaders must figure out how close to the edge of bankruptcy they want to be year after year. I do not believe that "faith" requires us to live a day or a week away from financial extinction; instead, I fall on the other side of the continuum. I like knowing that we could ride out a rough patch or two because we followed the example of the ant in Proverbs 6:6 and stored up a reasonable amount of reserves.

A pastor friend of mine is finishing a building program right now and at the end of it will be tens of millions of dollars in debt. His church has no reserves. None. He has been asking me questions along the way, and I keep saying the same thing to him: "Please be careful. Please build plenty of debt-reduction margin into your budget and some operational reserves so that you will be able to pay the mortgage even if the church goes through a difficult season."

"We'll be fine," he keeps reassuring me.

"And pay down that debt as soon as possible," I keep coaching him.

Over the years, I have lost my appetite for financial high-wire acts. I would rather build profit (reserves) into a budget and be able to give away a substantial amount of resources than spend the last thirty days of the fiscal year wondering if we might have to close up shop.

When our church was in its infancy, a board member said to me, "We should have a boiler fund."

I asked him what a boiler fund was, and he explained that years ago, families that owned businesses in Chicago found that when they ran too close to the financial edge, a big piece of machinery in their factory, such as the boiler, would decide to give way. Having no reserves to draw on, they couldn't afford to fix it, which meant they couldn't keep the plant running and would be forced to go out of business. Chicago folks started saying, "We need to have a boiler fund and keep pouring money into it, because someday when we least expect it, the boiler is gonna bust!"

That all made sense to me, but still I said to the guy, "We don't even have a building yet!"

"Listen," he said, "we *will* have buildings someday, and we'll have lots of big equipment that buildings require. On the day when a piece of that big equipment decides to blow, we'll all be glad we set aside funds for it now."

We have replaced several boilers over the decades (and roofs ... and air handlers), but never once did we have to traumatize the church when the equipment broke down.

If you and I really believe that the local church is the hope of the world, then I believe we should do everything in our power to make sure that, at least from a financial perspective, the ministry can thrive well into the future.

LINKS

#49 - IS IT SUSTAINABLE? [PG. 147]
#60 - PAY NOW, PLAY LATER [PG. 174]

12 | TAKE A FLYER

A wonderfully talented British film producer named Richard Curtis agreed to do an interview with me for a Leadership Summit session. In addition to writing and producing some of the best romantic comedies ever, he's also the brains behind the inception of Comic Relief UK, which last year surpassed the billion-dollar mark in terms of monies raised to fight extreme poverty. Amazing.

During our interview, Richard said something interesting about what it was like to get Comic Relief off the ground. He had been to Africa in the late 1980s and had seen firsthand the atrocities unfolding all around. He returned to England determined to give the next twenty-five years of his life to fighting disease and poverty and injustice.

The only thing he'd ever done professionally was to work with comedians and comedic scripts, so he decided he'd launch a wildly entertaining and hilarious telethon that would try to raise funds for those who were dying in Africa. "People thought we were *crazy*," he explained during our interview. "We were doing comedy and tragedy simultaneously, you might say, and the television executives didn't really have a category for that. But we knew the audience would respond, and well they did."

As I sat there listening to Richard recount his story, I couldn't help but smile. The guy had taken a flyer, and just as my experience could attest, many flyers wind up reaping huge rewards.

Throughout the course of his life, my dad built several different businesses but in doing so would always differentiate between "betting the farm" and "taking a flyer."

"If you bet the farm too many times, Billy," he'd say, "you'll eventually lose the farm. But if you take a flyer once in a while, you'll very likely come up with a breakthrough that could serve you well for a long, long time." *We take flyers. We don't bet the farm.* This was one of my dad's many mottos that has stayed with me my entire leadership career.

In the three-plus decades I've led Willow, I can honestly say that I have never bet the farm. Stories often surface about pastors who bet the farm and had things go right for them, but I never envy their gains or seek to emulate their decision making, because someday, if they keep rolling the dice, they'll lose the *kingdom* farm.

So from day one, I was determined to abide by my dad's flyer/farm policy. And wouldn't you know it: as far as Willow's experience is concerned, my dad's wisdom has been proven right. Over the years, we rolled out a highly controversial but extremely effective "seeker-sensitive" service. We incorporated the use of arts in worship services. We pioneered a new way to do small groups. We started a CARS ministry and a food pantry and a Spanish-speaking congregation. We employed team teaching from the main pulpit. We launched regional campuses. And just like Richard Curtis said, people thought we were crazy every single time.

Until these flyers worked.

In the course of a given month, I connect with probably a dozen local church pastors who want coaching or training in one aspect of leadership or another. On some occasions, they'll have me take a sneak peek at a strategic ministry plan they're about to roll out to their board or senior staff. And more times than not, I eyeball the plan and hand it back to them with a playful but dramatic yawn.

"Are you serious?" I ask.

After they affirm that indeed, they are serious, the next words out of my mouth are usually something like, "So let me get this straight: between now and next Christmas, you've got a grand total of *nothing* planned that is going to capture your congregation's imagination? I think you might be overdue for a flyer!"

I tell them that I think it might be time to get some of their church's fired-up Christ-followers in a room and ask what bold move they would make next ministry season if they knew that God would anoint it and bless it. "When God gives clarity to you," I continue, "thank him sincerely, figure out how to implement the move strategically in the life of your church, and then watch what God does!"

> "So let me get this straight: between now and next Christmas, you've got a grand total of nothing planned that is going to capture your congregation's imagination? I think you might be overdue for a flyer!"

My advice to them is my advice to you too, if your setting could stand a few sparks of God-ordained excitement: *Take a flyer!* It will keep you young, build your faith, and perhaps yield the breakthrough you need.

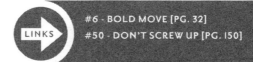

LINKS

#6 - BOLD MOVE [PG. 32]
#50 - DON'T SCREW UP [PG. 150]

13 | Vision Leaks

Some leaders believe that if they fill people's vision buckets all the way to the top one time, those buckets will stay full forever. But the truth is, people's buckets have holes of varying sizes in their bottoms. As a result, vision leaks out. You or I could deliver a mind-blowing, God-honoring, pulse-quickening vision talk on Sunday that leaves everyone revved up to go change the world, but by Tuesday, many people have forgotten they were even in church the previous weekend. Unbelievable, huh?

Something I have to remind myself of constantly is that people in our churches have *real lives*. You heard it here—engagements *other than* church. They have challenging jobs, children to raise, lawns to mow, and bills to pay. Because of all these daily responsibilities, the vision we poured into them on Sunday begins to drain out of them sooner than we think.

When you can tell it's time for a vision refill, use every communication means available to you to repaint the picture of the future that fills everybody with passion. And then take it a step further by reporting *progress* on the vision's achievement. Trust me, when you wrap a little real-life proof around the accomplishment of your church's vision and show that the dream really is coming true, the fog will start to clear and people's heads will start to nod. "Oh yeah!" they'll suddenly remember. "I get it! I get it! *This* is what we're about! *This* is why we exist as a church."

> *You or I could deliver a mind-blowing, God-honoring, pulse-quickening vision talk on Sunday that leaves everyone revved up to go change the world, but by Tuesday, many people have forgotten they were even in church the previous weekend.*

We've been lifting up the value of racial reconciliation at Willow for many years now. It's a central part of the vision God has called us to pursue. Nearly every time I close out a talk on the subject, I stand on stage in front of the whole congregation and say, "Now, Willow, as we go back out into our neighborhoods, our job sites, and our communities, let us be the *very first ones* in every social setting to reach a hand of friendship over a racial divide. This is part of who we are! We are the *first people* to bridge the racial divide."

A few months ago during our celebration of Martin Luther King Jr. weekend, we invited a member from a church on Chicago's south side to do an interview with a guy from our church. Like most everyone else, the two men had full lives and occupations and families to tend to. But over the course of several years, they carved out time to get to know one another beyond racial stereotypes. They took lots of emotional risks in their conversations, and eventually a deep friendship developed. Our leadership team hoped that the story would paint a vibrant picture of what it looked like to bridge the racial divide in everyday life.

I watched that interview from the monitor near my seat on the front row, and as the camera panned to various members of our congregation, I saw tears streaming down cheeks and obvious pride written on faces. "I love being part of a church where racial reconciliation is a high value," their countenance seemed to convey. "I love our vision! I love that we are actually achieving our vision!"

Ask key staff, "How full is your vision bucket these days?" Ask volunteers, "Do you sense progress around here toward our vision?" Ask members of your congregation, "Which part of our church's vision is the most meaningful to you?" Get a gauge on how full buckets are around you, leader, and then get busy topping them off.

LINKS

#5 - VISION: PAINT THE PICTURE PASSIONATELY [PG. 29]
#19 - INSTITUTIONALIZE KEY VALUES [PG. 67]

14 | VALUES NEED HEAT

What most people remember about high school chemistry lab is that for a few months, pyromania was actually legal. Still today, students the world over are encouraged to hook up a Bunsen burner, strike a match, and take some serious heat to whatever is in the beaker. I remember doing this in chemistry class and being awed as certain substances underwent dramatic changes in state as the temperature kept rising. There is an important leadership lesson to be gleaned from your old chemistry-class days, because values too need heat!

Many leaders gaze longingly at other organizations and wonder how values like innovation and teamwork and excellence became so prevalent there. They would pay huge sums of money to transport those values to their own organization, but they know deep down that it doesn't work that way.

Anytime you see God-honoring values being lived out genuinely and consistently, it's fair to assume that a leader decided to identify a handful of values and put a Bunsen burner underneath them. Every time she or he taught about the value or publicly praised someone for living that value out, it was like raising the temperature of that burner. Perseverance. Compassion. Servanthood. Generosity. Whatever the value, if it's alive and well in a local church today, it's not by accident. It's only there because of intentional, committed, dedicated effort.

> Whatever the value, if it's alive and well in a local church today, it's not by accident. It's only there because of intentional, committed, dedicated effort.

When you heat up a value, you help people change states. Want to jolt people out of business as usual? Heat up innovation. Want to untangle confusion? Heat up clarity. Want to eradicate miserliness? Heat up generosity! New "states" elicit new attitudes, new aptitudes, and new actions. It's not rocket science. It's just plain chemistry. Which is a lot about heat.

I was due to speak at a church conference one time, and as I drove onto the campus, I was greeted by a volunteer who offered to help me park my car.

I walked inside and was approached by another set of smiling volunteers who were anxious to point me in the right direction. Between talks, still another pair of volunteers made sure I had plenty of hot tea and sandwiches in my backstage room. I checked on a few resources at the book table and watched more volunteers serve customers with helpfulness and joy. No less than ten times that day, I was struck by the servanthood of this cadre of volunteers.

When the conference dismissed, the senior pastor walked me out to the parking lot. I had a feeling I knew why their volunteers were so terrific, but I posed the question anyway. "Just out of curiosity, how often do you teach on servanthood around here?"

He laughed and said, "Bill, it's the central thrust of my entire ministry! We talk about it all the time!"

Of course he does. Because no church gets a value *that* shockingly right unless the leaders diligently heat it up.

Pastors tell me, "You have such generous people at Willow!" as if we must have been on the lucky end of some random, cosmic congregational doling-out, while they got stuck with a slew of stingy types. It couldn't be further from the truth. A congregation is generous only because the value of generosity has been heated up.

Leaders must figure out what values they believe should be manifested in their organizations. And then put them over the flame of a Bunsen burner by teaching on those values, underscoring them with Scripture, enforcing them, and making heroes out of the people who are living them out. Over time, sufficiently hot values will utterly define your culture.

LINKS

#13 - VISION LEAKS [PG. 52]
#19 - INSTITUTIONALIZE KEY VALUES [PG. 67]
#24 - DNA CARRIERS [PG. 83]

15 | THE DANGERS OF INCREMENTALISM

A lmost all churches have one thing in common when they first start out: sky-high idealism. "We're not just going to impact our community or our city or our country," they cheer; "we're going to change the *whole world*!"

People pray big prayers, they give big dollars, they donate big-time hours, and they believe God is quite capable of doing absolutely *anything* through them. That is, until reality sets in. Over time, church leaders and congregations alike are dismayed to learn just how much energy and enthusiasm it takes to keep the machinery of a growing church chugging along. They become frustrated that they don't have adequate staff or volunteer support. They feel pinched on the resource front and struggle just to get bills paid each month. Slowly but surely, that "God can do anything" feeling fades, bold prayers quit getting prayed, and the beginning of the end is near. Without necessarily intending to, they drink the deadly hemlock called *incrementalism*.

You know you've ingested a little incrementalism when innovation is no longer welcomed in your environment. Blue-sky days? "Aw, they're a thing of the past." Taking a few flyers? "We don't even let the *youth* department do that anymore!" The biggest financial dream is a 3 percent increase over last year's income, because anything more than that would be going out on a *wild* limb of faith. Very slowly, and quite subtly, you find yourself increasingly satisfied with nothing more than incremental growth. And from there, things *really* start to go downhill.

> Slowly but surely, that "God can do anything" feeling fades, bold prayers quit getting prayed, and the beginning of the end is near. Without necessarily intending to, they drink the deadly hemlock called incrementalism.

I keep reminding pastors that the normal attrition rate for most churches is about 10 percent each year. That means you can be doing everything flawlessly—producing awe-inspiring worship services; effectively pointing people to faith and growing them up into dedicated followers of Christ; joyfully serving those who are poor; graciously providing shelter for those who are homeless; diligently caring for orphans and widows—and because of elderly people dying, career transitions, and people moving to new neighborhoods *alone*, you'll lose ten out of every hundred attenders each year. Toss in the shutdown of a manufacturing plant in your community, and that attrition rate could double.

You can understand my frustration, then, when pastors tell me they're "trusting God" for 3 or 5 percent growth this year. "Really?" I think. "That's tantamount to planning a funeral for your church."

Incremental thinking, incremental planning, incremental prayers—it's the kiss of death. Don't fall for it.

LINKS
#3 -YOU'RE ALWAYS IN A SEASON [PG. 24]
#12 - TAKE A FLYER [PG. 49]
#43 - A BLUE-SKY DAY [PG. 131]

16 | Six-by-Six Execution

I was sitting in an airplane one time coming back from an international trip, and the closer we got to Chicago, the more my mind swirled with the long list of to-dos awaiting my return. I took out my calendar and counted six weeks left until year-end. Only six weeks' time to tackle what seemed like a *hundred* critical challenges.

I grabbed a pen, took out an index card, and wrote one question at the top: "What is the greatest contribution I can make to Willow Creek Community Church in the next six weeks?" I wanted to know which decisions and initiatives only I could accomplish, which services we needed to hit out of the park, which staff issues I absolutely had to address, and so forth. It took me the better part of the remaining two hours of that trip to sort it all out, but the net result of that exercise was a list of six items that, if achieved, would have me singing the Hallelujah Chorus come December thirty-first.

The next morning, I placed that index card front and center on my desk. My list included things such as finishing my message for the Christmas Eve services, meeting a fairly large fund-raising challenge for one of our ministries, and hiring a key staff person. And by God's grace, over the next six weeks I got every one of those initiatives done. Candidly, I don't know that I have ever made a more significant contribution to Willow than I did those six weeks. But then again, I'm not sure I had ever been quite so focused in my attempts.

January rolled around, and I decided to do it once more. "Okay," I thought, "what are the six most important challenges I can focus on between now and the fifteenth of February?" I had another international trip coming up then and figured I'd feel like a war hero if I could go two-for-two on this newfound practice.

It took several hours of reflection to surface the top priorities, but once I did, I attacked them ferociously. In addition to dramatic increases in my satisfaction level because of all the work I was getting accomplished, I noticed my prayer life headed northward as well. I was crystal clear on what I was supposed to be doing for that six-week period of time, and I found myself shamelessly imploring God to show up and do mighty work on my behalf. Amazingly, he did just that.

In addition to orchestrating near-daily miracles around Willow pertaining to my top priorities, he also gave me a massive dose of peace regarding the *intentional neglect* of things that weren't on my beloved six-by-six list. It was during that season I learned that deliberate disregard can be every bit as important as conscious concentration.

I operated on my six-by-six plan for that entire calendar year and was so impressed by what my focused efforts yielded that at the next management retreat, I took two hours explaining the tool to my senior leaders. I allotted yet another two full hours for them to work through the exercise and net out their top six priorities. "There is nothing sacred about the six weeks," I explained. "But this past year, that particular amount of time seemed to keep my urgency level high. I can't sprint for six months, but six weeks? That, I can do."

There was also nothing sacred about having exactly six items on the list. Most leaders don't have the luxury of having only one ball to carry, but they know trying to juggle sixteen is an impossible feat. My teammates agreed that six seemed a reasonable compromise and were thrilled to finally have a streamlined set of goals to operate against. For twelve months straight, they did exactly that, emailing me their priorities one six-week chunk at a time.

> *"There is nothing sacred about the six weeks," I explained. "But this past year, that particular amount of time seemed to keep my urgency level high. I can't sprint for six months, but six weeks? That, I can do."*

The following summer, we upped the ante at the management team retreat. I said, "You've all done a fantastic job operating by the six-by-six tool, but I think it's time your peers see your cards, instead of just me."

All members of the management team — myself included — posted their most current six-by-six list on a flip chart and then, one at a time, walked their colleagues through the rationale behind their priorities. The drama that unfolded over the next two hours could have been a reality TV show. "*That's* not urgent!" someone would shout as he saw one of his peer's priorities. Or "Hang on a minute! You're focusing all your attention on *those* things?" another would ask, to the complete shock of the person who had written them down in the first place.

It was obvious there were varying opinions about what things qualified as the church's most pressing matters. The stunned person would say something like, "Well, surely you want me to focus on this!" and hear in reply, "No, no, no! Don't bother with that! Here, what if you focused on this instead. . . ."

We doled out revised task lists faster than a Vegas card dealer, and once the entire team saw the fruit of their collective labor, they sat back and said, "Now our next six weeks are going to be a ball!"

What's more, everyone was exposed to the sheer weight some of our team members were carrying. "Please know you're not in this alone," someone would say to a colleague whose list looked a bit intimidating. "The rest of us are going to be praying for you over this six-week period. If the load gets too heavy, let us know."

Staff leaders would see my list and say, "Bill, we had no idea you were pouring energy into all of that! How can we help? How can we pray for *you?*"

A really simple idea that had evolved into an effective management tool was now an informative, instructive, and corrective means of fostering a genuine sense of *team* among our senior leaders. Pretty cool.

We still operate this way today.

LINKS

#7 - AN OWNER OR A HIRELING [PG. 34]

#15 - THE DANGERS OF INCREMENTALISM [PG. 56]

#34 - DISAGREE WITHOUT DRAWING BLOOD [PG. 106]

#44 - THE BIAS TOWARD ACTION [PG. 134]

#47 - DOABLE HARD VERSUS DESTRUCTIVE HARD [PG. 142]

#58 - CREATE YOUR OWN FINISH LINES [PG. 169]

17 | ONLY GOD

It's the only phrase I intentionally overuse, but it's for good reason. When God accomplishes activity that no human being could possibly orchestrate, you have to respond somehow. And the simple phrase I've landed on in recent years is "Only God."

When I teach a message from Willow's main stage about what to do when your back is against a wall, and then say afterward, "I assure you I've got nothing better to do than stand right here and pray for every single one of you who feels your back is against a financial or spiritual or emotional or physical or relational wall," and then stay put for ninety solid minutes after three separate services as more than five hundred men and women step forward for prayer, I come away from that series of holy moments with but one thought in mind: "Only God."

When I see twenty-five hundred pastors and leaders in Lagos, Nigeria—a place recently named one of the "least livable places on planet Earth,"[6] and a place where I have *yet* to do a single promotional trip—gather for the Global Leadership Summit to learn how to cast vision and inspire teams and raise funds and reach irreligious people with greater effectiveness, there are just two words to sum it up: "Only God."

When I witness an amazing outpouring of generosity like I did last year at Willow's Christmas Eve services, where in a single week $1.1 million was given by one congregation to fight extreme poverty and HIV/AIDS all over the world, I can find only two words to encapsulate all that I am feeling: "Only God." Only God can touch thousands of hearts in such a way that people joyfully release what the world worships.

> *Only God can touch thousands of hearts in such a way that people joyfully release what the world worships.*

When by faith our church promises Habitat for Humanity that one hundred volunteers from Willow will gladly show up to their Benton Harbor, Michigan, Blitz Build to erect a series of homes for under-resourced families living there and then watch as 350 people raise their hands, take a week's vacation time from work, and jump into cars for the six-hour round-trip, we look at each other and realize for the umpteenth time that it wasn't the clever pitch or savvy wordsmithing that did it; it was only God.

When a hurricane called Katrina takes the lives of nearly two thousand Gulf Coast residents and I ask for three hundred men and women from our church to rally together and, taking limited vacation days from work, head to the devastated areas to pitch in, and more than *one thousand* immediately say "Yes, send me," I'm not at all sure how to respond except to shake my head and tell them one more time, "Only God."

When five of my colleagues and I head outside for a baptism service at the lake on Willow's campus and see three thousand people sprawled out on blankets ready to watch yet another thousand people get baptized, and the sky is blue and cloudless, and the New Testament is happening right here in the town of Barrington, Illinois, and collectively we know that what Christ-followers for centuries have dreamed of we are getting to see up close and personal as we ease one more head down into the water to acknowledge Jesus as Lord and Savior, we find ourselves speechless except for three simple syllables: "Only God."

Only God. It's more than an axiom. It is a theology that has been alive and well at Willow Creek Community Church since the beginning. We watch for our heavenly Father to move and stir and act and call. And when he does, we humbly thank him with the only two words that could even begin to give credit to the one to whom alone credit is due: "Only God."

LINKS

#20 - THIS IS CHURCH [PG. 68]
#42 - WE GOT TO DO THIS TOGETHER!
   [PG. 126]
#66 - TO THE CORE OF MY BEING [PG. 192]

plus-

18 | PLUS-SIDE/MINUS-SIDE

One thing you never learn in seminary is how to make a growing church economically sustainable. When I first started out in ministry, I had a general understanding that whatever the congregation put in the offering plate each week equated to the "available resources" we could use to build the church. What I *didn't* understand was that the manner in which I added staff members to our team would either dramatically help or dramatically hinder our church's overall financial viability. I had never heard anyone talk about this subject matter; like most of the church-work lessons I've learned, this one came the hard way.

In the early days of Willow, the initial group of staff we were hiring just happened to attract more families to our church. We added a children's ministry coordinator and a student ministries pastor and directors of evangelism and small groups. Without my even being aware of it, the more effectively these staff members did their jobs, the more we grew as a church. Almost immediately, there was an increase in offerings. By virtue of more people attending our church, more people were yielding their lives to Christ, more people were growing in their faith, and more people wanted to give God their tithes and offerings. Unbeknownst to me, my staff was contributing to the financial viability of our church, but I never connected the dots.

Over time, however, cries from the staff rang through the halls of Willow with ever-increasing volume: "We need more administrators!" "How about starting a missions department?" "When are we going to add more custodial help and data-entry support?"

I couldn't really argue. The roles being requested seemed necessary, and so we began to hire wonderful and talented people to fill them. A *lot* of wonderful and talented people. In the end, as you'd expect, our once rosy financial picture changed. The team members we added helped to accomplish the day-to-day operations of the church, but they did very little to boost our financial growth.

Things eventually became so bleak on the financial front that I rallied all the bright people I knew and asked for their opinions on what we should do. Nobody really knew, so one day I headed to a quiet restaurant to study the financial data and try to figure out the solution on my own.

The first thing I noticed was that our expense line was slowly beginning to outpace our revenue line. This had never happened before and of course captured my full attention. Why was this occurring when our offerings were going up? And why was this occurring when we were adding staff at approximately the same rate now as we had in the past?

Suddenly I grabbed a cocktail napkin, drew a fat vertical line down the center, and put a plus sign on top of the left column and a minus sign on top of the right. We had thirty-eight staff members at the time. "If each person were operating at their highest level of performance," I asked myself, "would their job fall on the 'adds dollars to the ministry at Willow' side of the equation, or would it fall on the 'consumes dollars' side?"

The children's coordinator role was an obvious plus. Because of that role, families felt comfortable coming to our church. They knew their children would be well cared for, and they liked the idea that they could enjoy a distraction-free worship service. As their commitment to Christ grew, so would their generosity.

The pastoral care counselor was probably a minus. While he did terrific work and had a great heart, most of the people he helped were troubled folks from our community who already attended other churches or who had sworn off church years ago.

I kept going down the list, slotting every role into one column or the other. Missions guy? Minus. In fact, from a pure financial perspective, the missions person was a *double* minus because, in addition to doling out a salary, there came a steady stream of requests to give increasing amounts of our church's money away. (A good and biblical thing when done wisely.)

Suddenly I grabbed a cocktail napkin, drew a fat vertical line down the center, and put a plus sign on top of the left column and a minus sign on top of the right. We had thirty-eight staff members at the time. "If each person were operating at their highest level of performance," I asked myself, "would their job fall on the 'adds dollars to the ministry at Willow' side of the equation, or would it fall on the 'consumes dollars' side?"

Accounting people? Well, they *counted* the money, but unless they were cooking the books, they probably weren't adding a lot to the revenue stream.

Twenty minutes into this exercise, I felt like a creep. I couldn't believe what I was doing, but I saw no other way to help our church climb out of this hole than to distill everything down to this one incredibly irreverent exercise. And honestly, the results were profound. All those recent staff hires I had made — every single one of them — fell on the minus side of my napkin. There were the names, all fifteen of them, clear as day. I immediately realized that if I stayed on this same path without a keen awareness of the plus-side/minus-side dynamic, I would single-handedly imperil the future financial health of the church we all were so passionate about building for God's glory.

I was so excited about my breakthrough that afternoon that I did a very unwise thing. I headed back to the church, hurriedly called a staff meeting, and announced to everyone that, after careful analysis, I had finally discovered the truth behind our financial crisis. (I knew they'd be so pleased!)

I re-created my napkin art on a huge chalkboard, complete with a plus on one side, a minus on the other, and every single staff member's name listed in big, bold letters. Once and for all, we'd all be able to see which roles were adding to the financial health of our church and which were sucking us dry.

"Gang," I said with passionate enthusiasm, "I've just been adding too many 'minus-side' folks to the mix without balancing them out with enough 'plus-side' people! I'm so sorry! I'll rectify this immediately, and in the future, I'll take this into consideration as we add staff!"

Whew! What a narrow escape for our little church. In light of my confession, I just knew my staff would be as relieved as I was that we had finally cracked the code on our financial crisis. Now we could all live happily ever after!

The shocked and terrified looks on everyone's faces told me that they were not as sure of their futures as I was.

After an awkward silence, our missions pastor raised his hand. "Yes?" I said.

"Uh, Bill, correct me if I'm wrong, but you *hired* me to give away lots of money. It's kind of ... it's my *job* to give away money, and now I'm being fired for it?"

His questions opened a floodgate, and in five minutes flat the entire room had dissolved into a pool of panic and fear and frustration. "How can you get rid of us?" the minus-side people burst out. "We are working every bit as hard as the plus-side ones!" "Doesn't an Acts 2 church require some people whose jobs will *always* be to route resources to the poor?" "Are we going to pay plus-side people more than minus-side people now?"

To say I backpedaled would be a gross understatement. "No, no, no," I ventured. "You misunderstand me. It's not *bad* if you're on the minus side. It's just something that our senior staff has to keep in mind as we add folks to the mix. We must put some plus-side people into the equation, or else we'll fold as a church."

In addition to learning a very important "financial fact of life" about church economics that day, I also learned which discussions should be held in front of the full staff and which should be worked through in church boardrooms. Live and learn. But beware of plus-side/minus-side dynamics. They are real!

LINKS

#3 -YOU'RE ALWAYS IN A SEASON [PG. 24]
#49 - IS IT SUSTAINABLE? [PG. 147]
#52 - FACTS ARE YOUR FRIENDS [PG. 155]

19 | INSTITUTIONALIZE KEY VALUES

Thanksgiving Day has single-handedly institutionalized the value of gratefulness. In America at least, it's nearly mandated that once a year—predictably toward the end of November—you'll stop whatever you're doing and just say thanks all day long. Brilliant!

The same thing happens with Christmas, Good Friday, and Easter. These regularly scheduled holy days force us to raise the value of the incarnation, atonement, and resurrection each and every year.

I thought about this type of thing many years ago and wondered if there were other key biblical values that we could institutionalize and lift up every year by attaching them to a holy day sometime in the church calendar year. So we experimented.

These days, everyone in "Willow World" knows that on Martin Luther King Jr. weekend we are going to lift up the values of radical inclusiveness and racial reconciliation. On World AIDS Day—always occurring the first weekend of December—everyone knows that we are going to remind our congregation of the plight of people trapped in generational poverty and suffering from HIV/AIDS. On Mother's Day and Father's Day, we are going to make huge investments in our parents.

What you value in your church must be raised up, taught about, and celebrated on a regular basis.

The key learning is this: What you value in your church must be raised up, taught about, and celebrated on a regular basis. And to force yourself to honor key values annually, you must institutionalize them somehow. Trust me, this works!

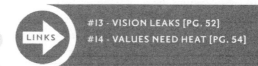

LINKS

#13 - VISION LEAKS [PG. 52]
#14 - VALUES NEED HEAT [PG. 54]

20 | THIS IS CHURCH

It's Thursday. I'm in the middle of a hectic week, and my phone rings. It's a Willow dad whose son was just arrested. "Bill, can you come meet me for a cup of coffee?" I know this guy well. He wouldn't interrupt my day unless something big was going down.

I drop everything and drive over to the restaurant, my curiosity growing as each mile passes. He seemed very intense on the phone.

The restaurant is empty except for the booth where this dad sits, his elbows on the table, his head in his hands. I sit down across from him and look at him and listen carefully as he begins to speak. He's efficient, even in his evident grief.

I'm hearing his every syllable as the Spirit whispers in my ear, "This is church."

That whole thing I'm trying to build back at the office by hiring staff and funding facilities and approving ministry programs is at its best when it is distilled into this one single moment in a Greek restaurant when one need is being met in the life of one individual who matters immensely to God. We must all stay mindful of this.

It's Sunday. Everyone has been prepped, the logistics have all been handled, and as I walk out of the eleven fifteen worship service toward the lake, I see scores of Creekers pressed against the shoreline, eagerly anticipating today's baptism of hundreds of men, women, and children. As I near the water, I'm pulled aside by a man I recognize instantly. Thirty years ago, I led this guy to Christ and baptized him in these same waters.

Years later, I'd help to lead his son to Christ and then baptize him here too.

Today, he tells me, his grandson now wants to be baptized. He wants to know if there is any way that I can do the honors. Administrators are vying for my attention, the other teaching pastors are already waist-deep in the lake, and the congregation is antsy to get going.

I keep my eyes trained on this man's face, determined that, despite the other things I need to be tending to, this moment will not be lost on me. Three generations of men whose lives have been beautifully wrecked by grace. And God allowed me to play a role in the whole deal. "This is church," the Spirit whispers as tears fill my eyes. I say to this man, "Keep your grandson near you until we have finished everyone else. I'll baptize him myself at the very end."

It's Tuesday. My leadership team and I are in a staff meeting, and we need to get started. The agenda is ambitious, and the clock is ticking.

We spend the first few moments checking in with each other, and we learn that just this week, one of our teammates' parents has had to go into long-term care. She explains that she and her husband and her siblings feel as though they're booting their father out of the family. She felt extremely guilty on the drive over to the facility that her dad is now supposed to call home. The emotional roller-coaster, despair, and disillusionment she was juggling were almost too much for her to bear.

I look at the eyes around the table and glance at the blank flip-chart pad that's standing at attention, all ready to go, and the Spirit whispers yet again, "This is church."

What's happening *right now*, this is what church is all about. Even amid a Very Important Meeting during which we plan to solve Very Important Problems, I remind myself that the whole reason we show up for these meetings, the whole reason we do *anything* around here, is to create an environment where people who are elbowing or wrestling or weeping their way through seasons of disappointment can receive ministry.

Christ said he was going to build "his church" — a community of real people with real, beating hearts that would be attentive to each other and responsive to each other and quick to extend mercy and grace and love.

Even amid a Very Important Meeting during which we plan to solve Very Important Problems, I remind myself that the whole reason we show up for these meetings, the whole reason we do anything around here, is to create an environment where people who are elbowing or wrestling or weeping their way through seasons of disappointment can receive ministry.

I find myself all throughout my week being reminded of what actually defines church. It's not some amorphous or corporate-feeling organization that I'm spending all these hours trying to fix or to advance. It's a living, breathing, pulsating organism that is evolving real-time based on the thousand ways we choose to care for each other, listen to each other, hold each other up when the rug has just been yanked out from beneath our feet.

Interdependence, vulnerability, listening, giving of ourselves. Can you hear the Spirit whisper to you now? "*This* is church."

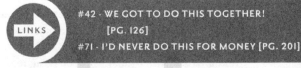

LINKS

#42 - WE GOT TO DO THIS TOGETHER! [PG. 126]
#71 - I'D NEVER DO THIS FOR MONEY [PG. 201]

s church

teamwork & communication

the

The Three Cs

It took me nearly thirty years to figure out a plan for how to build a kingdom dream team—a collection of colleagues with whom I could joyfully do effective, God-honoring ministry over the long haul. I tried all sorts of mental grids for prioritizing people-qualities along the way, but the only one that stuck was made up of three simple Cs: character, competence, and chemistry.

> *I tried all sorts of mental grids for prioritizing people-qualities along the way, but the only one that stuck was made up of three simple Cs: character, competence, and chemistry.*

It's no accident that "character" is up first. When new staff members come on board, I need *maximum* energy, *maximum* effort, and *maximum* help from them. Most likely, the reason the person was hired in the first place is because there are problems that have to get solved in order for kingdom ground to be gained. If the first ninety days of a person's employment are frittered away because I'm forced to do a character reclamation project on his or her life, then we're all in big trouble.

Good character is tough to discern in a fifteen-minute interview. You have got to do your due diligence to be sure the person you're about to invite onto the team has a proven track record of being a truth-teller, a covenant-keeper, a person who seeks to be conformed to the image of Christ, someone who manages relationships well, and one who credits the efforts of others when a victory is won.

After a person passes the character test, and *only* afterward, I check for competence. When I'm working to fill a key role, I think through the competency requirements. If I need someone with a teaching gift, then I make no apologies for scouring the planet for the best teacher I can find, and then I go after that person with great determination.

I've found that persistence is often the key here. If someone tells me no, I can't let it deter me. I must keep the conversation alive by seeking to truly understand the other person's perceived obstacles and then, depending on how badly I need them on board, doing everything in my power to help overcome them. I counsel senior leaders in this regard all the time. They ask me how long they should pursue the person who is "perfect" for a particular role, and my response is the same every time: "How many lunches are you willing to buy?"

Unless God gives you a clear signal to stop, my advice is to keep extending the invitation.

John Ortberg was one of the finest team members Willow ever had, but when I first approached him with the teaching pastor opportunity, he said no. I probed a little further, and he said, "Bill, the main reason I can't come is because I have only been at my present church for two years. To leave now would be unfair to our people."

I told him that was the best news I'd heard all day. "Great! I understand perfectly. So in twelve months, then, you'll join us? We would be delighted to wait that long. We believe that you are the best fit for our needs."

A little over a year later, John joined us and served heroically for almost ten years.

Never apologize for looking for maximum competence in your new teammates, gifts and talents and capabilities that will take your ministry to the next level of effectiveness. But before you agree to hire them, be sure to run them through the chemistry screen.

I used to be a doubter when it came to emphasizing "fit" when hiring a new staff person. If they nailed the character requirement and had competence to spare, I was quite sure they would do fine. They'd learn to mesh with the existing team and me once they were on board. Not always so. I learned the hard way to trust my gut on this: if I get negative vibes the first two or three times I'm in someone's presence, it's likely I'm not going to enjoy working with that person day in and day out. Sounds crass, I know, but I have learned this painful lesson too many times.

I presented this framework at the Leadership Summit one year, and in response I got a batch of letters from pastors and business leaders who totally disagreed with what I'd said. "You shouldn't decide about a person based on how well they fit with the other team members," one said. Another claimed that "competence ought to go first, because you can smooth out the character stuff over time."

Within a few years, however, most of them had written to me again — this time to ask for a copy of that Summit talk. Nearly all of them had charged ahead and hired someone who didn't fit the three-C grid—or who didn't fit the three items in the right order—and had paid dearly for the decision. I smiled when I got that second batch of letters because I could relate all too well to what these leaders were walking through. After cleaning up my share of royal messes, I finally reached the point where I decided I would never knowingly violate the three Cs again.

LINKS

#8 - HIRE TENS [PG. 38]

#22 - NEVER SAY SOMEONE'S NO FOR THEM [PG. 78]

#23 - FIRST TESTED [PG. 80]

#29 - SPEED OF THE LEADER, SPEED OF THE TEAM [PG. 94]

#42 - WE GOT TO DO THIS TOGETHER! [PG. 126]

three cs

22 | NEVER SAY SOMEONE'S NO FOR THEM

We're trying to fill several key staff roles at Willow right now, and recently one of my associates came into my office to give me a progress report. He got to one of the positions on his list and said, "You know, I was thinking about going after so-and-so for this role, but there's no way he would come. It's really too bad. He'd be perfect for this!"

It's an odd tendency I see in even the most discerning and faithful leaders: when they're trying to add a great board member or an elder or a small group leader or other key leader, they ask God who would be the *very best person* on planet Earth to fill the position. Upon receiving the answer, they proceed to pursue everyone but that individual. In almost every case, the "very best one" is a fantastic leader who is already busy doing extraordinary work somewhere else. "That" person might have to agree to a pay cut to join our team. "That" person might have to relocate from some balmy utopia to the Midwest ... and surely they won't do all that just to come serve alongside us.

For these reasons and many more, we take them off our wish list. Then, realizing we can't have our top pick, we drop down a few levels and begin to consider the folks we *can* have. Sure, they don't have the skills and competence of our number one choice, but hey, at least they're available. This is a problem.

It takes a lot of discipline to approach wish-list people, but some of the most exceptional employees

> It's an odd tendency I see in even the most discerning and faithful leaders: when they're trying to add a great board member or an elder or a small group leader or other key leader, they ask God who would be the very best person on planet Earth to fill the position. Upon receiving the answer, they proceed to pursue everyone but that individual.

we've known are people who sat across the table from me one time when I said, "I know this is a long shot, and this may be a very short conversation, but would you pray about joining Willow's team? I think you are the absolute best person for a critical position we are trying to fill. I know you have some exciting things going on already. And frankly, I was tempted to say no for you, but then I realized that maybe it's something God would have you pursue. At a minimum, I wanted you to know of the opportunity. Please pray about whether or not it's for you."

On more than one occasion I have been shocked and delighted when extremely talented people called me and said, "Count me in!" I was so glad I hadn't said their no for them.

We had a big transition at the top of a ministry department one time, and the perfect person to fill the slot was right in our own backyard. He attended Willow and was a faithful, high-capacity volunteer, but the guy had just started a business and was pulling in more than two hundred grand a year. Our salary offer would be just a *tad* bit less than that. Still, I met with him and cast my most passionate vision for the role he would play.

Several days later, he called and said, "Bill, by human standards, this is the stupidest decision I could ever make. But it's a yes. God spoke to me. I'm in. I'm going to sell my part of the business and give you and Willow five years of my very best efforts." He did just that and left behind a strong legacy that remains to this day. Things don't always pan out like this, but in my experience, nothing is ever lost by leaving room for the surprising and supernatural emergence of a yes.

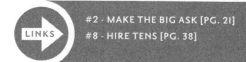

LINKS   #2 - MAKE THE BIG ASK [PG. 21]
         #8 - HIRE TENS [PG. 38]

23 | First Tested

"What's the biggest mistake you've ever made as a leader?" It's one of the most frequently asked questions I've received since I began coaching pastors and church leaders.

My answer's always the same: "Placing people in significant leadership roles who were not first tested." Truly, most of the worst managerial calamities I've caused—ones in which people got deeply hurt—can be traced back to my being overly optimistic putting people in roles they were ill equipped to play.

More times than I care to admit, I shouldered people with meaningful ministry responsibility before I'd adequately assessed their spiritual depth, their relational savvy, their capacity to operate effectively within a team environment, and their ability to deal with a crisis. Time and again, a stiff penalty was paid by all.

But how do you find leaders in the making?

In 1 Timothy 3:10, it says that if people want to lead in the church, "they must first be tested." And so, in deference to those five critical words, I began to establish experiments that would "first test" young men and women I thought might become leaders someday. I'd ask them to pitch in and solve a few practical problems around the church so I could watch how they responded to a challenge, how they established the trust of a team, and how they navigated difficult situations when they arose. (And they *always* arose.)

Most of the worst managerial calamities I've caused—ones in which people got deeply hurt—can be traced back to my being overly optimistic putting people in roles they were ill equipped to play.

A few years into my experimentation, a generous man gave Willow Creek some money earmarked for building a camp in the north woods of Michigan. On a fairly consistent basis, I would approach eight or ten prospective leaders whom I barely knew and say, "Think you could help the church out with a project up north?"

I'd load up those willing souls in a van and head to the Upper Peninsula for four or five days of backbreaking work as we cleared trees and hauled materials we'd use to erect rustic cabins and a dining lodge. Sure, we were building a camp, but I had ulterior motives. I was testing leaders I had brought with me to see who rolled up their sleeves and who wandered away. Who stacked firewood so others had decent showers and who stood under the hot water for an hour, oblivious to what that did to the woodpile.

Camp Paradise would emerge from all those months of hard work. But equally important was the intangible by-product that showed up: a lifelong leadership lesson that told me *never* to put someone in a significant leadership role until first testing them — up close and personal.

As Willow expanded over the years, my experiments expanded too. For example, I took teams of people on sailing trips with me. Few secrets remain, about anybody or anything, after spending seven straight days together on a forty-five-foot boat. Those sailing trips provided me with more critical insights into developing leaders than any other environment. On a sailboat, once dinner is done and the dishes are washed, all that is left to do before going to bed is to talk. And talk we did — for hours.

Other times, I took people on the road with me. What did they do when their baggage was lost? What did they say when a hotel reservation was cancelled? How did they behave in unguarded moments?

Sometimes I put people on ad hoc task forces just to see how they would respond in a team environment. We hosted a huge outreach event at Willow one time that involved putting on a community-wide production. The show included original music and scriptwriting, and we believed it held great promise for our church. In fact, by God's grace, we wound up impacting upwards of forty thousand people over the course of eight performances.

About three weeks before opening night, we entered stage rehearsals. I was asked to provide feedback on how the program was looking, but instead of attending alone, I decided to ask a random assortment of high-potential leaders to come with me. Ostensibly they were there to provide input on how we could improve the performance, but I was doing a discernment check on all of them.

To my surprise, despite my assumption that *all* of those twelve men and women qualified as potential elders or board members, the net result of that particular test was a grand total of one. Sure, the others were seasoned enough, strategic enough, and kingdom-minded enough to help our church in other areas, but in my judgment, only one of them was ready for a big role at Willow. I was so glad I had arranged that test!

Still today I manufacture multiple tests for almost every leader who might wind up with significant responsibilities at our church. It requires a ton of work, but the payoff is huge. I challenge you to do the same: run a few "first-test" experiments, and see if they help you too.

LINKS

#7 - AN OWNER OR A HIRELING [PG. 34]
#8 - HIRE TENS [PG. 38]

24 | DNA Carriers

Let's say you wake up tomorrow and decide to start a car dealership. Now, because you're ever the overachiever, this won't be just *any* car dealership. No, this dealership will trump every other dealership in existence. This dealership will treat people with honor, respect, and understanding. Prices will be fair. Service will be thorough. Communication will be clear. And follow-up will be speedy.

You start making plans for how these operating values are going to get lived out. Jolts of excitement course through your veins as you consider the vast possibilities. "We'll allow extended test drives!" you think. "We'll provide upscale loaner cars when clients' cars need maintenance! We'll make personal phone calls to people after we service their cars to be sure everything is working properly and all of their questions are answered!"

You're destined for success, you believe, because you're determined to be a car dealership with a conscience. This is the dream you're chasing, and this will be the key differentiator between your store and all others in town.

So you start your business and rejoice in the fact that everything is unfolding beautifully. That is, until you hire your first batch of employees. They don't carry the same dream. They don't possess the same level of passion. They can't for the life of them understand why you blow a gasket every time they accidentally forget to make their follow-up calls.

What's the source of the problem here? The employees? Maybe. But perhaps the *real* culprit is the fact that you're carrying the organization's DNA alone.

Great leaders know that when they assemble teams around them, they can't merely assign tasks for people to check off a list. Instead, they

Great leaders know that when they assemble teams around them, they can't merely assign tasks for people to check off a list. Instead, they must launch an all-out DNA-infusion campaign to make sure everyone is on the same "values" page.

must launch an all-out DNA-infusion campaign to make sure everyone is on the same "values" page.

Great leaders take the time to explain to their team what they feel deeply about—what issues they would take a bullet for and why. Then great leaders show their staff members how to live out that DNA. They appeal to the employee's desire to be part of something very cool and then make a hero out of each one who rises to the occasion. Sure, the final decision rests in the hands of the employee—"Will I or won't I live out all that it means to be part of this organization?"—but effective leaders challenge and inspire their staff to become bona fide DNA carriers.

Not surprisingly, Jesus was the master when it came to this. He played out countless scenarios with his followers in order to reinforce the values he believed must characterize his kingdom movement. Through his actions, Jesus showed his followers that things such as courage and humility and perseverance would be rewarded. And that selfishness and pride and judgment would not. (The Pharisees had to hate that day when their rock-throwing plan was deterred and an adulterous woman walked free.)

Jesus affirmed those who were making DNA progress and reprimanded those who were headed in the wrong direction. I think back to Matthew, whom Jesus praised for enfolding his sin-scarred, tax-collecting buddies mere hours after he himself crossed the line of faith. "Well done, Matthew," Jesus probably said. "Compassion, inclusion, Spirit-led action—you're a DNA carrier through and through."

How inspiring to hear these words from your leader!

Admittedly, Jesus had the luxury of building a ground-up operation. It's not as if he took over the church after the predecessor had made a mess. He was rather like the founding pastor, and whether or not that is true for you too, you're not off the DNA hook. If you did not have the joy (or the pain!) of starting your organization yourself, my advice to you is to study the history and identity of what occurred in the organization before you arrived. It had some values: carefully discern which should be honored and carried into the future. Bless the people who have been living them out. Then, when the time is right, begin teaching everyone what the new DNA will look like.

I visited a cathedral recently in Durham, England, with a few WCA staff members who had joined me for that leg of the trip. The place had been there for nearly a thousand years and just oozed history. On our way out, one of my colleagues smiled and said, "Hey, Bill, what would you do if you were anointed bishop here tomorrow?"

"Brand-new bishop of a thousand-year-old church," I said. "Well, I'll tell you what I *wouldn't* do. I *wouldn't* trot out some new vision my first week on the job. That would be pastoral suicide! I'd study the history of that congregation until I knew it better than anyone in the place. Then I would affirm every praiseworthy part of that history. It might take months to accomplish, but so be it. Only after everyone knew that I valued the past would I begin to infuse the people with the DNA that I felt would take us into a God-glorifying future. And with God's help, who knows … the next thousand years might see that church catch its stride!"

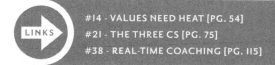

LINKS

#14 - VALUES NEED HEAT [PG. 54]
#21 - THE THREE CS [PG. 75]
#38 - REAL-TIME COACHING [PG. 115]

carriers

teamwork and communication | 85

25 | No Eleventh-Hour Surprises, Please

L eadership is supposed to be a forward-looking process. Part of what this means is that leaders like to know about problems while they're still small so those issues don't grow into big, organization-imperiling monsters that can kill momentum and threaten mission achievement. Leaders like to be *prepared*. They like to have contingency plans A, B, and C mapped out so that pitfalls can be avoided and the opposition can be defeated. This is what leaders were made by God to do.

One of the most harmful things a colleague can do to a leader, then, is to toss an eleventh-hour surprise in his or her lap. Last-minute grenades ask an otherwise proactive person to become reactive, a well-paced problem solver to become a firefighter, and a long-term planner to focus all energies only on the next twenty-four hours.

I caught my fair share of grenades in the early days of the church. I'd entrust ministry budgets to staff members, only to come within days of the end of our fiscal year and be told, "Oh, by the way, I'm going to be seventy-five thousand over my budget this year." My frustration level would spike instantly. Surely this was a personal betrayal. "How *could* you?" I'd mutter as the grenade-tosser walked out of my office.

> *Last-minute grenades ask an otherwise proactive person to become reactive, a well-paced problem solver to become a firefighter, and a long-term planner to focus all energies only on the next twenty-four hours.*

The board of directors meeting would arrive, and I'd be the one taking responsibility for the colossal miss. "If my colleagues had just given me more time to react to their bad news," I'd think, "I could have put together a plan for mitigating the effects or even turning the situation around altogether." When you take the time advantage away from a leader, you limit his or her ability to resolve problems.

Many years ago, Willow's then-CFO came into my office and told me right before year-end that we were going to have a near-million-dollar "insurance problem." The board reacted exactly how a board should, and I reacted worse than that.

The next day, I paid the executive a visit in his office to ask one simple question: "How long did you know about the shortfall?"

"Six months" was his answer.

Six months!

Maybe he hoped the rapture would come before I found out—I don't know. All I know is that because he chose to stay underground with his information, our entire organization was thrust into a full-blown fire drill.

Eventually I developed an axiom around this concept that I conveyed to everyone on my senior staff team. "No eleventh-hour surprises, gang. Deal? In fact, let's shoot for no *tenth*-hour surprises and see how that goes for a while."

I explained to them that if they saw something leaving trend line, I wanted to know within *days* of the departure. "If I know about something early enough, I can probably assemble a team to ameliorate the issue. Can we all agree to this?"

It would be difficult for me to describe how much stress this principle has removed from my life. I have gone so far as to ask staff members who are contemplating transitioning off of our staff to give me as much notice as possible. This provides us with more time to be able to identify a replacement with minimal trauma to our ministry.

The "no eleventh-hour surprises" value is something the point leader has to instill consistently in *all* followers so that it eventually becomes a cultural norm. Beat the drum loudly and as often as you have to: "I want an environment that helps keep blood pressure stable, the nuttiness quotient low, and fire drills and soap operas to a minimum. *Please*, no eleventh-hour surprises."

#31 - DELIVER THE BAD NEWS FIRST [PG. 99]
#39 - JUST TO BE CLEAR [PG. 117]

LINKS

26 | How Are You Doing ... Really?

In American culture, when you ask people how they're doing, they're nearly always "fine." So if you want to convey that you are actually interested in hearing the truth about what's going on in that person's inner world, and if you want to give the other person permission to answer you honestly, then you have to pose the question just a bit differently: "How are you doing ... *really?*"

I don't want ministry to become so professional and efficient that the stuff of relationship and community gets squeezed right out. It would be a travesty to spend half a day in meetings with a colleague and then find out later that she'd slept in an ER by an ailing family member's side the night before. Could I not have taken thirty seconds out of the agenda to see if she and the other team members were okay that day? If one of my teammates is worried or frustrated or distracted in some significant way, then I want to know that. And not just for leadership's sake, but for love's sake too.

Simply put, your followers have to know it's legal to admit that while they may be sitting across the conference-room table wearing a smile and a trendy outfit, nothing is fine or fitting quite right on the inside.

In Galatians 6:2, the apostle Paul says that we fulfill the law of Christ when we agree to "carry one another's burdens." The people you lead have to know they're part of a burden-carrying team. They have to know there's an avenue for them to convey whatever personal or professional calamity they face. They have to know they can trust their colleagues to hear them out. Simply put, your followers have to know it's legal to admit that while they may be sitting across the conference-room table wearing a smile and a trendy outfit, nothing is fine or fitting quite right on the inside.

An approach I have taken thousands of times over the years is to set aside the first few minutes of my weekly senior leadership team meeting to get a read on each person's emotional state. I'll say something like, "Gang, we're going to spend the next three or four hours together working on some big issues that face our church. But before we dive into the tasks at hand, I'd like to go around the circle and have each of you answer the question, 'How are you doing . . . really?' I know you all *look* great, but are you really *doing* great? Give the rest of us a minute or two of insight into that question, and then we'll tackle the business issues we need to tackle."

Often we start around the circle and the first person says, "How am I really doing? I'm good. I had a fantastic private time with God this morning, my relational world is rich, I'm feeling strong and energized about the things I'm involved in, and I'm glad to be here with you all. I'm good."

The next person takes his turn. "How am I doing . . . really? Well, not that great, to be perfectly honest. Right after this meeting, my wife and I are taking our son to see a specialist. Things aren't any better on the health front, and I'm pretty weighted down in my spirit."

Once everyone has had a turn, we pray for each situation—the good, the bad, and the ugly. The experience doesn't take that long, but the result is significant. As we move into the business portion of the meeting, we feel understood as individuals and unified as a team.

Years ago, one senior leader on our team had three teenage sons who were all great kids deep down but limit-pushers by personality. Each week he'd entertain us with their latest acts of terror; eventually I'd bait the update by kicking off the meeting with, "Well, what did Bobby smoke this week?" We'd all have a good laugh, but beneath all the kidding around, he knew our care was sincere. He knew that we wanted his family to win, and in a strange way, I think joking with his teammates about the struggles he and his wife faced in raising their boys gave him added strength for the journey.

Another of our colleagues walked through the loss of her aging father in full view of our team. Over a long five-year period, the situation digressed from her stopping by his home every night to feed him, to moving him into a retirement community, to hiring assisted-living care, to having to wipe drool off his face as he slumped in his wheelchair, to near-fatal falls and other emergencies. Every one of us attended her dad's funeral. We sat right by her side, which is where we'd been since day one. What an honor. To this day, she says those short bursts of dialogue about the most important thing going on in her life were balm to her heart every single week.

Sure, you'll have to limit the "talkers" on the team, draw out the quiet types, and rally near-supernatural strength to encourage ones who have been dealt a leveling blow. But as you work to create an atmosphere of genuine community, you'll keep your hearts tender toward each other, you'll keep your collective prayers more focused, and you'll keep the "church" in church work.

LINKS

#30 - PAY ATTENTION TO GREETINGS
AND GOODBYES [PG. 96]
#42 - WE GOT TO DO THIS TOGETHER!
[PG. 126]
#56 - SPEED VERSUS SOUL [PG. 166]

27 | Get the Right People around the Table

Many people would gasp in horror if they knew how many times a major challenge has faced Willow that I, as the senior-most leader, had no clue how to solve.

More than three decades ago, we started the church and immediately needed a facility where we could hold weekend worship services. I was new to the community and had no idea how to secure a facility. But I was quite confident we'd find a place to call home.

Years later, we needed land so that we could operate from a permanent location. I knew very little about land acquisition, but again I was quite confident things would work out.

When we were finally prepared to build our first building, we needed to get financing and go through a zoning process. I'd never once experienced a zoning hearing and had no clue about the finer points of construction finance. Would everything come together? I was sure it would.

Many people would gasp in horror if they knew how many times a major challenge has faced Willow that I, as the senior-most leader, had no clue how to solve.

As the years went by, our church navigated all sorts of uncharted waters. There were suicides and divorces and lawsuits and wrecks and, one time, even a burglary. Someone broke into our accounting area where weekly tithes and offerings were kept overnight and actually stole the safe with the weekend offering in it. That was a memorable middle-of-the-night phone call.

I could go on and on with examples, but the point is this: when a really tough situation presents itself and you're the leader in charge, what do you do when you don't know what to do? Each time, instead of bluffing my way through or flipping a coin or having a meltdown or quitting, I'd simply resolve to get the right people around the table. I figured if the right people were around the table, surely God would speak through them or through me or through our collective conversation and show us which direction to head.

Get the right people around the table. I believe in this principle like I believe in gravity. I really do think that every serious problem known to humankind is addressable and solvable when the right people are invited into the dialogue.

Isaiah 54:17 promises that no weapon formed against us will prevail. I take that verse to mean that with heaven's help there is absolutely no reason bright, godly people can't solve any issue that threatens to trip them up.

It's part of the great drama of leadership very few people understand, this idea that, in any given situation, one person can utter one sentence in one particular moment that simply stops time. Everyone in the room is halted by the feeling that, finally, the intense fog is lifting. You never know when that one great breakthrough is going to show up, but what high adventure it is to stick in there until it does! Often after a meeting where we experience a breakthrough, I drive home thinking, "I never would have expected that particular person to catalyze the breakthrough, but wouldn't you know it? That's exactly who God used to do it. No doubt about it, that woman was the right person to have at the table today."

There are still dozens of very complicated and seemingly unsolvable problems on my leadership plate today, but I get up every morning with the confidence that if a bunch of smart people who love God, love the church, and love each other will devote adequate time to these problems, there's no mountain we can't move.

LINKS

#10 - THE VALUE OF A GOOD IDEA [PG. 42]
#43 - A BLUE-SKY DAY [PG. 131]

28 | KNOW WHO'S DRIVING

Near the top of almost every meeting I attend, I ask the question, "Who's driving?" I don't ask for my benefit alone; in full view of the other participants, I want to get someone on the hook for running a successful meeting. I want someone to declare that he or she is, in fact, in charge of the meeting. This person will lead us with confidence and will ensure the thorough discussion of the entire agenda and will manage the energy and pacing of the meeting. This person also will take responsibility for the inclusion of the slow-processors and the quieting down of the "quick-talkers," as my friend Henry Cloud calls them, and will call fouls when they are committed.

Who's driving? It's a critical question to ask before the meeting starts, and it's a critical question to revisit as the meeting is coming to a close. Before dismissing any work session of substance, I look at the person who was in charge and say, "You were driving this meeting, right? So are you going to make sure that the assignments are accomplished and that follow-up happens as it needs to?"

> *If no one claims to be driving, then seldom will anything of consequence occur.*

If no one claims to be driving, then seldom will anything of consequence occur. Get someone to go on the record from the get-go. You won't regret it.

One final thought on this concept. In the early days of Willow, the question "Who's driving?" rarely had to be asked. I am embarrassed to say that I was the self-appointed driver of almost every meeting.

As I matured as a leader, though, I began to see that letting other people "drive" meetings was a critical part of their leadership development. These days, the reason I have to ask who is driving as often as I do is because I am trying to raise up dozens of skilled drivers in our ministry. Might it be time to do the same in your context?

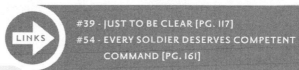

LINKS

#39 - JUST TO BE CLEAR [PG. 117]
#54 - EVERY SOLDIER DESERVES COMPETENT COMMAND [PG. 161]

teamwork and communication | 93

29 | SPEED OF THE LEADER, SPEED OF THE TEAM

The most powerful two-word leadership phrase Jesus ever uttered was "Follow me." The apostle Paul told believers to imitate him just as he imitated Christ.[7] *Follow me, imitate me*—both statements refer to the power of leading by example.

A series of questions lurks in the minds of followers—questions that can best be answered simply by observing their leader. When followers wonder how joyful they should be about their work, all they should have to do is observe their leader's joy level. "How joyful is he?" they ask themselves. "How joyful is she? Because that's how joyful I will be!"

When they wonder how determined they should be in their jobs, all they should have to do is observe their leader's level of determination. "*That's* how determined we'll be!"

When they wonder how much credit they should give to others when good ideas get implemented, when they wonder how gracious they should be to their peers, when they wonder how quick they should be to admit their mistakes, when they wonder how much faith they should have, all they should have to do is look to their leader, and those followers will have their answers. Right?

Leaders must never expect from others anything more than they're willing to deliver themselves. They should never expect higher levels of commitment, creativity, persistence, or patience than what they themselves manifest on a regular basis.

> *If you cannot say, "Follow me," to your followers—and mean it—then you've got a problem. A big one.*

If you cannot say, "Follow me," to your followers—and mean it—then you've got a problem. A big one. Speed of the leader, speed of the team.

"Follow my values. Follow my integrity. Follow my work ethic, my commitment, and my communication patterns. Fight as I fight. Focus as I focus.

Sacrifice as I sacrifice. Love as I love. Repent as I repent. Admit wrong as I admit wrong. Endure hardship as I endure hardship." When requisite actions back them up, these are the words that set followers' hearts soaring.

#7 - AN OWNER OR A HIRELING [PG. 34]
#54 - EVERY SOLDIER DESERVES
        COMPETENT COMMAND [PG. 161]
#65 - LEAD WITH ALL DILIGENCE [PG. 190]
#74 - ADMIT MISTAKES, AND YOUR STOCK
        GOES UP [PG. 209]

30 | PAY ATTENTION TO GREETINGS AND GOODBYES

Leaders are driven by causes that affect them deeply. They see people living on the street and have to provide resources. They see people suffering with treatable diseases and can't help but hunt down medicine, as well as find a way to get that medicine to those in need. They see wanderers who have given up on God and will turn over heaven and earth to accompany those folks back home.

Indeed, part of the wiring pattern of leaders is that they have a huge bias toward action. As a result, most of them get up every morning with freshly stirred, God-given passion for moving every player in their organization one step closer to mission achievement.

It stands to reason, then, that a leader sometimes seems to be three-fourths steamroller and only one-fourth caring and compassionate colleague. When a leader walks into a meeting, for example, he or she usually has only one thing on the brain: *mission advancement.* There are problems to solve, strategies to create, resources to raise, and personnel fires to douse. Naturally, because the leader's mind is singularly focused on "task," the other people in the room can be easily overlooked. When the hour strikes, the gavel is pounded and the leader is ready to get down to business. It's just a leader's nature.

I've been in several hundred meetings with other leaders, and I can usually predict the language the leader will use as the meeting time draws near:

"Ready to get going?"

"Shall we start?"

"Let's dive in."

"I'll open with prayer, and then we'll get after it so we don't waste anyone's time."

I get a kick out of it every time I hear this "let's roll" language because I used to do the same thing around Willow. That is, until I shared a cab one time with a leader I deeply respect. We were halfway into our trip to the airport when he turned to me and asked me the strangest question: "Bill, do you know what the most important part of any meeting is?"

I could think of several right answers: The agenda. The decisions. The outcomes. "This must be a trick question," I thought. "What's he driving at?"

Before I answered, he said, "You probably think it's the agenda, but it's not. Bill, my friend, the most important part of every meeting is your greeting and goodbye."

"Why would you say that?" I asked.

"Bill, everyone who works for a highly motivated leader carries with them a low-grade concern that that leader is going to use them and then toss them out. They worry that aside from getting the leader's agenda done, they're not at all necessary. Deep down, they simply want to know that they're more than just a cog in someone else's wheel."

He went on to explain that although he could be characterized as an activistic leader, he had established a practice that helped him counterbalance his overemphasis on task and convey care to the board members and colleagues with whom he worked. "I make it a habit to do a personal, enthusiastic, genuine, warm, highly relational, look-you-in-the-eye greeting to every single person sitting around the table before I even *think* about starting the meeting."

"I make it a habit to do a personal, enthusiastic, genuine, warm, highly relational, look-you-in-the-eye greeting to every single person sitting around the table before I even think about starting the meeting."

As if that weren't enough, he told me that he paid equal attention to the very *last* thing that happened in the meeting room. "That's what people will remember," he said. "So when I adjourn a meeting, I go to the doorway as soon as I can to give a warm thank-you to every member as they leave. No matter how intense the meeting was, they are given direct assurance that I was grateful for their contribution."

I remember being quite impressed when I heard this leader's take on greetings and goodbyes, but I wouldn't know the power of his perspective until I tried it on for size myself. My board members unwittingly served as my guinea pigs. At our next several meetings, I greeted them warmly. And individually. And while looking them in the eyes.

After the meeting, I said goodbye with handshakes and sincere words of thanks. Wouldn't you know it, almost immediately our board meetings improved: attendance went up, morale went up, the spirit with which we conducted our business was better, and the reticence a few of them had about continuing on as members dissipated into thin air. They were all changes that I could trace back to my greetings and goodbyes. Try it.

LINKS

#26 - HOW ARE YOU DOING . . . REALLY? [PG. 88]

#42 - WE GOT TO DO THIS TOGETHER! [PG. 126]

#56 - SPEED VERSUS SOUL [PG. 166]

#66 - TO THE CORE OF MY BEING [PG. 192]

31 | Deliver the Bad News First

I f you are your organization's primary mouthpiece, this small but important communication tip will be your friend: Always deliver the bad news first.

I've learned the hard way that what you leave with someone at the end of any given communiqué—whether written or verbal, whether in large groups or small—sets the tone for how they feel about the future of the organization or endeavor.

If I have five major pieces of information to tell my board or the congregation or my senior staff team and two of them are on the difficult side, those are the two I lead with. "I've got a handful of things to convey, and the first couple are going to be tough to hear," I'll say. "I don't want to pretend otherwise." Then, not in a shaming or blaming way, but in a clear, concise, nothing-but-the-facts manner, I'll explain what has gone awry and why. "This ministry is behind plan," or "We fell short of our goal by 50 percent in the first half of the year."

Once the bad news is out, I am freed up to shift to an upbeat posture. "On another note, I've got some great news to report about a couple of other things...."

Then, before dismissing everyone, I summarize what we've covered in a positive way: "To recap, these are some things that we can't rejoice about just yet. But please hear me straight out: we are still moving into the future in full-trust mode with God, believing that he is going to do something fantastic in and through our efforts."

I've seen too many leaders kick off a meeting by rattling off their best news first, and then, just before adjourning, they say, "Now before I let you go, we really need to talk about one issue in particular." They trudge through all the gory details of the team's failing, close with an ominous-sounding prayer, and leave everyone dejected because all they can remember of the meeting is that "one issue" that was such a downer at the end.

The difference between great communication and not-so-great communication often comes down to where you place the bad news. Sure, it has to be covered. But as the leader, try delivering that first. Get it over with, and then get on with something that will leave your people in a much better place.

The difference between great communication and not-so-great communication often comes down to where you place the bad news.

LINKS

#30 - PAY ATTENTION TO GREETINGS AND GOODBYES [PG. 96]
#52 - FACTS ARE YOUR FRIENDS [PG. 155]

32 | THE TUNNEL OF CHAOS

One of the greatest contributions author and psychiatrist M. Scott Peck made to this world was to shine a spotlight on the differences between participating in genuine community and experiencing what he coined "pseudo community."

If community involves things such as knowing and being known, serving and being served, loving and being loved, and celebrating and being celebrated, then most relationships, Peck asserted, are constantly devolving into pseudo community. It's the great temptation for small groups of people to slide into a state where they're not *quite* telling each other the truth and they're not *quite* celebrating each other. Instead, they tolerate each other, they accommodate each other, and they settle for sitting on the unspoken matters that separate them.

Years ago, what captured my imagination about Peck's concept was the aha that in order to move from pseudo community to genuine community, you have to endure a little chaos. To break free from falsehood, someone has to upset the applecart and say out loud, "As far as I can tell, we're not experiencing real community here. We're not where I want for us to be,

> *It's the great temptation for small groups of people to slide into a state where they're not quite telling each other the truth and they're not quite celebrating each other.*

anyway. Frankly, I'm holding back. I'm not giving you the final 2 percent of what I'm thinking. And I'm not really hearing what you have to say, either."

When I taught on this idea at Willow, I drew two circles on a flip chart and labeled the one on the left "Pseudo Community," the one on the right "True Community."

"We all want to get to true community," I said, "but we find ourselves in pseudo community. So how do you move from one place to the other?"

I added another element to the drawing, a tunnel that connected the two circles. "You have to be willing to go down into a tunnel," I explained, "a tunnel called chaos."

As I continued, I asked the congregation to think of the three most important relationships in their lives, such as those with their spouses, family members, close friends, or business partners. "How many of you know that you're settling for pseudo community with at least one of those three people?"

More than half the crowd raised their hands—quite interesting, given the fact that nobody in his or her right mind actually *wants* to live in less-than-true community.

We settle for pseudo instead of demanding the real deal for one simple reason: fear. "What if airing the issue actually make things worse?" we think. "What if probing the situation only serves to ruin the relationship?"

To these fears and more, there's only one response: the tunnel. Frightening as it is to enter that tunnel, those who do are the ones most likely to pop up one day into the fresh, life-giving daylight of true community.

I've been in hundreds of pseudo-community situations in which the only option was for me to invite the other person down into the tunnel. We'd be sitting across from each other in a restaurant, our food would have been served, and there would come that awful and awkward point when there was nothing else to say except the one thing that had to be said: "This is quite likely going to be a difficult conversation," I'd start, "but I'm committed to working this through no matter what it takes."

And then the back-and-forth would begin as we both recounted the steps that had led to our relational demise: "I meant this," and "You said that," and "Here's where I think we lost our way."

Chaos would actually be a tame way to describe some of the exchanges I've experienced in this regard. Sometimes it all feels downright scary. It's messy. It's ambiguous. It can be ugly. But it is almost always worth it.

Recently one of my ministry cohorts came unglued during a creative session. We were trying to finalize some video footage, and right after I gave a few minutes of candid input on her work thus far, she burst into tears. The response was atypical, so immediately I knew something else was fueling such a dramatic display of emotion. There was an awkward silence for a few minutes as I sat there wondering what to say or do.

I prayed a quick prayer for wisdom from God and then asked the only question I could think to ask: "What's it like to be sitting in your chair right now?"

She explained the frustrations she was feeling and the stress she had been under, and suddenly I realized she had been in a jam for quite some time. "How terrible it would be to feel that alone and that overwhelmed," I replied.

We went on to talk about where the train had left the tracks and what we could do to get it headed in the right direction once more. In half an hour's time, all was well again. But had we not been willing to dig down into that tunnel of chaos where tough questions demand candid answers, there might well still be tension between us today.

Ministry is a series of battles, and a lot can get said on the front lines that may not be exactly edifying. Every leader must constantly ask direct reports, chief lieutenants, key donors, and the best volunteers, "Are we okay? How can we clean up the messes we've made along the way?"

Stay prayed up, rested up, and committed to entering the tunnel of chaos whenever the Spirit prompts. It's one of the truest tests of character and love.[8]

LINKS

#36 - HELP ME UNDERSTAND [PG. 110]
#42 - WE GOT TO DO THIS TOGETHER! [PG. 126]
#57 - DID WE DO ANY LEARNING? [PG. 168]

33 | JUST SAY IT!

People who work in Christian settings often feel obligated to present opinions with a level of politeness that can often dilute the point they are making to where it is barely recognizable. The other people in the room respond with blank stares, wondering what in the world this person has just said.

Often, the weird silence lingers until some brave soul finally pipes up. "Huh?"

The original speaker panics. "Oh no," he thinks. "I must have offended someone with my comments. I'd better take another run at what I was trying to say, but this time, I'll be even more careful!"

He nervously delivers his watered-down spiel all over again, this time with added cushioning and broadening and hemming and hawing. Eight long minutes later, his peers are even more confused.

Good leaders just don't let stuff like this happen. Even if they have to interrupt the person midsentence, the best leaders I know refuse to tolerate mushy communication. Instead, they say, "Time is valuable and we all have lots to do today. It's obvious you have something on your mind, so I'd like to give you total freedom right now to come out and just say it. We are all big boys and girls who actually enjoy candor, but we can't make any progress on your proposal until you make it clear. So once again . . . just say it!"

Thirty-three years into my ministry run, I still find myself having to speak those words. Which goes to show how much effort a leader must expend toward creating an environment where people feel safe enough to speak clearly and directly to the group at large.

If your teams are like mine, from time to time you'll detect occasions when it's not just one person tiptoeing around the truth, but the entire group. My advice is to nip it in the bud. Stop the

> *Even if they have to interrupt the person midsentence, the best leaders I know refuse to tolerate mushy communication.*

meeting, tell the team you sense something lurking in the shadows of their communication, and get a pulse-read on each and every participant. Say, "I'd like to hear from everyone around the circle in a straightforward way. Please give the rest of us your ten-second reaction to what has unfolded here in the last half hour, no more and no less. Don't sermonize, edit, or hide. Just come right out and say it!" It is amazing how much time you will save and how many of your colleagues will thank you after the meeting.

LINKS

#36 - HELP ME UNDERSTAND [PG. 110]
#41 - KEEP SHORT ACCOUNTS [PG. 123]

teamwork and communication |

34 | DISAGREE WITHOUT
DRAWING BLOOD

Author Catherine Johnson wrote a book fifteen years ago titled *Lucky in Love*. She's a Ph.D. who was determined to figure out what deliriously happy married couples were so deliriously happy about. So she interviewed them—about a hundred couples in all. Want to know the one key learning she made? She found that at some point along the way, every happy couple had come to a critical point in their relationship where they covenanted together that they would *vociferously disagree* but *refuse to destroy each other* in the process. They could give you the time, date, and location when they finally established that no matter how difficult the conversation, they simply would not verbally attack each other. "When we quarrel (and we will!), we're not going to do the kinds of things that will damage this relationship long-term," Johnson quoted these couples as saying. "When we disagree, we will not draw blood."[9]

The moment I read that phrase, I decided to put it into practice in my work as well as in my marriage. Because I have deep feelings about so many kingdom issues, I have been known to express myself very passionately in meetings. And as you probably know, passion can beget passion. Effective leaders do not fear passion. They welcome it. But from time to time passionate discussions digress into personal attacks, and real people get really hurt. In my view, leaders must head that off before it happens. Your team must know that as the leader, you will never sit idly by and allow a meeting to turn into an alley fight.

Recently in a large public forum, a man asked me a question that was so sarcastic and mean-spirited that our security team rose to the ready. I have been through this kind of thing many times, and so reflexively, I asked the rest of the people in the room to quiet themselves before I addressed the verbal terrorist himself. I said, "In golf, when a player hits a terrible tee shot, his friends may be gracious enough to give him a mulligan, a do-over shot with no penalty attached to it. Just pure grace. Now, sir, your question was clearly a personal attack aimed at me without a shred of evidence to back up what you're saying. I'm willing to answer your question honestly right here in front of everybody, but only if you are willing to restate it in a kinder way." The crowd erupted in applause.

The man took a minute to rephrase his question, and upon asking it far more civilly the second time, the applause was deafening. Our congregation will remember that moment for a long time.

Once the "disagree without drawing blood" language is ingrained in a culture and the senior-most leader insists on enforcing that value it represents, a kind of protection is provided for everyone.

The Ephesians 4 "truth in love" passage starts off with Paul telling Christ-followers to "live a life worthy of the calling you have received." He runs through what makes up this type of life, things like humility, gentleness, patience, and *peace*. Leader, insist on leading in a manner that contributes to unity, even in the heat of disagreement.

Effective leaders do not fear passion. They welcome it. But from time to time passionate discussions digress into personal attacks, and real people get really hurt. In my view, leaders must head that off before it happens.

#33 - JUST SAY IT! [PG. 104]
#37 - LEADERS CALL FOULS [PG. 112]

35 | UMBRELLA OF MERCY

Creative meetings are often dangerous places. A leader stands up and says, "Okay, team, we have an event to plan [or a problem to solve or a new series to launch], and we need our most creative thoughts. Remember, there are no bad ideas! Let's just throw everything out there, because even an idea you think is bad may well lead to the one good idea we need."

It's standard language for these types of settings, and while the leader may genuinely believe there are no bad ideas, followers assume a big risk when they float one that might fit the dreaded description. In almost every creative session I've been in, at one point or another, someone had an idea that they wished they could surface but just couldn't muster the courage to get it said. Rather than face ridicule or eye-rolls or, worse yet, criticism from their colleagues, they opted instead to keep it underground.

Years ago, Nancy Beach, Willow's longtime head of programming and production, brought the "umbrella of mercy" concept to one of our creative meetings.[10] Just before communicating a possibly unworkable idea, she placed cupped hands over the top of her head like a charade umbrella and said, "Give me a little mercy here, okay?"

The practice caught on immediately. During future brainstorming sessions, one simple gesture afforded the speaker just enough courage to get out his or her idea, no matter how wacky or impractical it seemed, and move confidently through the brief period of emotional risk they'd stepped into. "Give grace, not judgment"—this was the agreement we struck whenever we saw a team member pull out the umbrella of mercy.

In almost every creative session I've been in, at one point or another, someone had an idea they wished they could surface but just couldn't muster the courage to get it said. Rather than face ridicule or eye-rolls from their colleagues, they opted instead to keep it underground.

I've found the practice useful not just in brainstorming sessions, but at any meeting where I need to float an idea that feels emotionally risky. At some meetings, I'll not only signal the umbrella of mercy to everyone in the room, I'll also make each person look me in the eye and promise *individually* that they'll treat my fledgling idea carefully. And only when they all give assent will I proceed.

Truly, some of our all-time greatest ideas have surfaced in those umbrella-of-mercy moments. We may look stupid doing it, but it's one of the smartest signals we ever implemented in our culture.

#10 - THE VALUE OF A GOOD IDEA [PG. 42]
#43 - A BLUE-SKY DAY [PG. 131]

36 | HELP ME UNDERSTAND

The huge temptation for a leader when a subordinate makes a mistake is to launch into the "what were you thinking" spiel, especially when a core value of the organization is violated. But you and I both know that approach can be degrading to the direct report and potentially dishonoring to God.

A little tool I started using to control my passion when confronted with costly mistakes was to begin the conversation with the words, "Help me understand."

I'd get wind of a student ministries volunteer loading up ten kids in the back of a pickup truck and joy riding around the church campus at high rates of speed "just for grins." He would be invited to sit on the other side of my desk, and I would say, "Please help me understand what you had in mind here. Maybe you were just trying to transport the kids across campus — you weren't aware of how fast you were going or someone else reached their foot over and pushed the accelerator to the floor, I don't know. Why don't you help me understand what really happened...."

A little tool I started using to control my passion when confronted with costly mistakes was to begin the conversation with the words, "Help me understand."

Or I'd learn that a young sound technician wanted to find out how far he could push one of our sound systems before the speakers blew up. He found out, to the tune of several thousand dollars. Hmmm ... "Please help me understand!"

Obviously the main reason I use this tool is to avoid slipping into an accusatory role or inadvertently polarizing the conversation before I fully understand what actually transpired. Certain things don't make sense to me and seem terribly unwise on the surface, but if the other person is given freedom to help me understand the situation, maybe I can see the situation from another angle. Seventy-five percent of the time, I still wind up pursuing the same course of action in response to the information I learn, but the spirit of the exchange is altogether different. Try these three simple words. You might end up using them as often as I do!

#24 - DNA CARRIERS [PG. 83]
#38 - REAL-TIME COACHING [PG. 115]
#50 - DON'T SCREW UP [PG. 150]
#57 - DID WE DO ANY LEARNING? [PG. 168]

37 | LEADERS CALL FOULS

I spend most of my life in meetings, so I'm quite motivated to make them as effective and enjoyable as possible. But by definition, meetings involve people. And lots of people means lots of personalities. And occasionally — just *occasionally* — those personalities clash.

I've seen my fair share of these clashes in meetings where I wasn't the one in charge. Flagrant interpersonal fouls that were obvious to everyone in the room would get committed and go unchecked. Board meetings would go bad, staff meetings would stalemate, and "team-building" retreats would degenerate into all-out junk fests. And yet nothing would be done. Everyone in attendance would sit there thinking the very same thing: "Why doesn't someone call a foul?"

These terrible experiences served to intensify my commitment to calling fouls in settings where I *was* the one in charge at a meeting. Still today, if someone gets a bit too cross on my watch, I don't hesitate to call a time-out and remind the offending party that in meetings I chair, there are ground rules to follow. I'll often say, "I don't know how things go in other situations, but when I'm in this seat, we will all speak to one another with respect. We won't interrupt each other, and we won't belittle each other's ideas. Instead, we're going to listen to each other attentively. We are going to choose our own words carefully so that the process will be as God-honoring as the outcome."

> *Board meetings would go bad, staff meetings would stalemate, and "team-building" retreats would degenerate into all-out junk fests. And yet nothing would be done. Everyone in attendance would sit there thinking the very same thing: "Why doesn't someone call a foul?"*

Effective leaders call fouls. They call fouls when unhelpful words are spoken. They even call fouls when no words are spoken at all. A colleague of mine used to use strong body language to keep our entire team from making progress. Through nonverbals like folding his arms across his chest, rolling his eyes, and staring out the window during group discussions, he conveyed exactly where our meeting fell on his list of priorities.

He knew he was sending a signal, but when I confronted him, he had the nerve to look me in the eye and plead innocence: "But I didn't *say* anything!"

Body language often becomes the elephant in the room—the enormous issue *everyone* can see and hear and smell—and if it's not addressed immediately, everyone suffers.

If someone is persistent in committing fouls, then I'll stop the meeting and say, "We don't have to take any additional group time to tackle this, but can you stay afterward so we can talk about a few things?" Everyone knows what is going to happen after the meeting: their teammate is going to get some personal coaching. But hopefully everyone also knows my goal is to improve our group dynamics.

For years I led a creative team meeting each week, and each week we would kick things off with a brief time of prayer. One of the guys on the team loved to pray, so nearly every week he would be the one to pray first. This would have been fine, except that his prayers were deflating and demoralizing to the entire team. He'd say something like, "Oh God ... [insert dramatic pause], we are all so tired and exhausted and overwhelmed and weary. We all have so much on our plates, and none of us really wants to be in this meeting right now. But here we are, and so would you please give us the energy to get through it?"

It frustrated me for months, but is it legal to call a "foul" on a prayer?

I decided it was. I pulled him off to the side one afternoon and said, "Listen, when you talk to God in private, it's perfectly appropriate to do the Psalm 62:8 thing, pouring out your heart to him. But I want to ask you to reflect on how wise it is to project your personal misery on the entire group at the beginning of a creative meeting. In my view, your prayers have been so demotivating that I am very close to asking you to help us all ... by *not praying*!"

To say the guy was offended by my comments would be an understatement. "Who are *you* to edit my prayers?" he scoffed.

It was a fair question. "You're probably right," I admitted. "I can't actually edit your prayers or keep you from jumping in during the prayer time. What I *can* do is disinvite you from the meeting. The choice is yours, but either way, this pattern cannot continue. Are we clear?"

Even though he stayed quiet during prayer times after that, I eventually decided to put him on another team. Shortly after that, he left our staff of his own volition.

Calling fouls is the responsibility of the leader, but you don't have to bear the burden alone. If you are faithful to model the calling of fouls consistently, the time will come when your team will not only help you call fouls, but they will also begin to call their *own* fouls. When that day arrives, you will know that great strides have been made.

LINKS

#28 - KNOW WHO'S DRIVING [PG. 93]
#34 - DISAGREE WITHOUT DRAWING BLOOD [PG. 106]
#36 - HELP ME UNDERSTAND [PG. 110]
#41 - KEEP SHORT ACCOUNTS [PG. 123]

38 | REAL-TIME COACHING

Years ago I served as the chaplain for the Chicago Bears. Periodically I would go to practices, and when I did, I was always intrigued to see how the coaches and players interacted. For instance, there would be a linebacker coach who would run all of the linebackers through a series of intense drills. Partway through, he'd stop the play, gather everyone around, and explain what they were doing wrong and how they could do better. Then he'd fire up the drill again and watch for improvements.

What struck me is that the coach didn't wait until after practice to have these interactions; instead, he provided real-time coaching so that his players could get better as quickly as possible.

I've tried, though imperfectly, to prioritize this same commitment to real-time coaching in my leadership. If I notice something going awry on one of my teams, I try to figure out a way to question or coach someone right there on the spot, rather than wait for a formal evaluation time scheduled days or weeks in the future. While this approach seems time-consuming in the moment, it has long-term payoffs that are hard to beat.

If I notice something going awry on one of my teams, I try to figure out a way to question or coach someone right there on the spot, rather than wait for a formal evaluation time scheduled days or weeks in the future. While this approach seems time-consuming in the moment, it has long-term payoffs that are hard to beat.

I was with a good pastor-friend of mine at his church recently, and halfway through the service I leaned over and asked how he was feeling about the energy level in the auditorium. "I'm worried about it," he admitted. "The service is almost half over, but it feels like everyone's still asleep!"

I asked him what he thought was contributing to the collective lethargy, but he couldn't put his finger on it. "If you're open to an outside opinion," I said, "I think your stage lighting might be the culprit."

The stage was drenched in dark greens and reds with not a single hot blue or vibrant white to be found. "In my opinion," I said, "you've got to draw people's attention to the onstage action the minute the service begins or you might never get them back." Because he seemed open, I added, "It also seems like the sound system is muffled. With a little adjustment between services, I think a brighter sound mix will add lots of life to the next gathering."

Later that afternoon, while en route to the airport, he said, "Bill, thanks for speaking at our church this weekend. I'll remember a lot of things from our time together, but the thing I'll remember most is that you *coached* me, right there in the front row of our worship service. I can do for my entire team exactly what you did with me, and we'll all be better for it. Thanks."

Real-time coaching is not my original idea. While Jesus walked planet Earth, his leadership style was undeniably characterized by the propensity to stick his team members in challenging, real-life situations and then affirm them for what they did right and coach them when they needed a little redirection.

One of the greatest gifts a leader can give to colleagues and direct reports is immediate input. Don't wait seven days, or even seven hours, to point out what's working and what's not. When things are going right, immediately say, "Great job!" And when things aren't going so great, quickly offer up some coaching to get things back on track. Your team will thank you for it.

LINKS

#41 - KEEP SHORT ACCOUNTS [PG. 123]
#44 - THE BIAS TOWARD ACTION [PG. 134]

39 | JUST TO BE CLEAR

There was a period during World War II when Great Britain was being bombed night after night, leaving an entire country left to wonder whether they were supposed to endure further attack or wave the white flag of surrender. As the air raids continued, there was a growing yearning among the populace to hear from their leader. One day, Prime Minister Winston Churchill addressed the nation. "We shall defend our Island, whatever the cost may be," he said. "We shall fight on the beaches, we shall fight on the landing grounds, we shall fight in the fields and in the streets, we shall fight in the hills; we shall never surrender."[11]

Now, some people may not have expected or even agreed with Churchill's decision that day, but *no one* could say he was unclear. He played a certain trumpet with his words, its sound perfectly clear to every listening ear.

When Dr. Martin Luther King Jr. was organizing civil rights marches in the 1960s and registering African Americans by the hundreds to vote, a group of influential leaders tried to calm him down. In their view, Dr. King was a bit too activist for their taste. "Just wait a little longer, Dr. King," they pleaded. "Whites will start treating blacks better. Really. Give them a little more time. Just wait."

Dr. King was in a prison cell in Birmingham, Alabama, when he received that "just wait" message.

He delivered a message of his own in response.

> We have waited three hundred and forty years for our constitutional and God-given rights, [wrote King]. Perhaps it's easy for those who have never felt the stinging darts of segregation to say "Wait," but when you have seen vicious mobs lynch your mothers and fathers at will and drown your sisters and brothers at whim; when you have seen hate-filled policemen curse, kick, and even kill your black brothers and sisters . . . when you have to concoct an answer for your five-year-old son's question, "Daddy,

why do white people treat colored people so mean?"; when you take a cross-country drive and find it necessary to sleep night after night in the uncomfortable corners of your automobile because no motel will accept you; when you are humiliated day in and day out by nagging signs reading "white" and "colored"; when your first name becomes "nigger" and your middle name becomes "boy" ... when you are forever fighting a degenerating sense of "nobodiness," *then* you will understand why we find it difficult to wait.[12]

He was absolutely and fearlessly clear: "No more waiting. We are marching. Today."

He blew a certain trumpet from his jail cell that day, the reverberations of which served as a crucial turning point for the entire civil rights movement.

One of the most consistent cries I hear from church attenders all over the world is the cry for clarity from their pastors. It's the cry for a *certain* trumpet sound from their church leaders. It's the cry that says, "Look, there are a dozen things we could be doing on Sunday mornings, but we choose to be part of God's church. We get the kids up. We make the drive. We sit here, all suited up, ready to run this way or that. Tell us to charge, tell us to retreat ... just tell us! And please make it *clear*."

One of the most consistent cries I hear from church attenders all over the world is the cry for clarity from their pastors. It's the cry that says, "Tell us to charge, tell us to retreat ... just tell us! And please make it clear."

Great leaders know they must be *crystal clear* with their trumpet sounds. And a practical way this gets worked out is in our day-to-day communications with those we lead. The more experience I get under my belt regarding organizational communication, the more I realize that it's just not enough to state something clearly and then assume that everyone understands. You'd think that would suffice, but it doesn't.

At this stage in my life and leadership, I now know I have to go back yet again and add the "just to be clear" step. "Just to be clear, here's what I meant." Or "Just to be clear, I'm asking you *not* to do this, and I *am* asking you to *please* do that." Or "Just to be clear, we agreed I'd have your report on Tuesday, correct? As in, *this* Tuesday?"

I take this third step as often as possible and even request it in writing from time to time. Yet I'm still amazed by how often I wind up in communication breakdowns with people who love God, love Willow, and love me. It is just the nature of the beast in a complex, fast-paced organization. If there is an ounce of wiggle room, things will inevitably wiggle the wrong way.

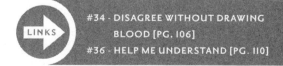

LINKS

#34 - DISAGREE WITHOUT DRAWING
BLOOD [PG. 106]
#36 - HELP ME UNDERSTAND [PG. 110]

40 | GIVE ME AN A, B, OR C

A tale of communication gone awry: A small-groups pastor works full-time for his church and is an all-around great guy. He thinks he's doing a fine job recruiting, training, and deploying small-group leaders just as he was hired to do, but right before Christmas the senior pastor calls him into his office to say that he has some bad news. The small-groups area has not been meeting the expectations of senior leadership and he will have to be terminated.

The small-groups pastor's jaw drops.

"You had no idea this was coming?" asks the senior pastor. His incredulity is tough to conceal as a nasty little thought races through his mind: "The fact that you had no idea you were about to be let go only further validates my belief that you are completely clueless about your effectiveness—or lack thereof—in this role!"

The shocked and saddened guy sits there staring into space as he hears his boss continue. "Listen," the senior pastor says, "I'm afraid we need you to clean out your desk and vacate the premises before the Christmas Eve services, so we can start fresh with someone new in January."

Disillusioned and very angry, the fired small-groups pastor heads home that afternoon and gives his wife the painful blow-by-blow of the day's events. The following night at an already-scheduled meeting for all the small-group leaders in the church, he tells the five hundred people in attendance the whole sordid story. Soon enough, the senior pastor's phone is logging scores of calls from staff and key volunteers and congregation members alike, not with Christmas greetings, but with demands to know how a debacle like this could happen in a church.

I wish this story were a work of fiction, but it's not. I've heard it recounted in various forms in hundreds of churches all around the globe, Willow included. And after living with a squishy personnel evaluation system for far too long in our own environment, I finally decided to take drastic action.

The result? Yearly "staff evaluation dialogues," as we call them. They take at least an hour per person, they cover a half dozen cogent points of discussion, and they result in a letter-grade ranking for all staff members so that they know exactly how they're doing. An A, a B, or a C—you can argue with the approach, but you can't argue with the fact that it's clear. In the U.S. culture, at least, *everyone* knows what these marks mean: "A" means excellent—you're exceeding expectations; "B" means good; and "C" means improvement is needed soon.

When I first implemented this concept, it was unpopular with nearly everyone on our staff. But the clarity of its output has eventually overcome whatever discomfort it originally caused the people who work at Willow. Author and consultant Patrick Lencioni says that many organizations are infected with "terminal niceness," which nets out in the inability to tell the truth to each other. I knew that if we didn't establish a system whereby meaningful, candid evaluations were given, underperformance would be tolerated and our ministry would never live up to its redemptive potential.

> *I knew that if we didn't establish a system whereby meaningful, candid evaluations were given, underperformance would be tolerated and our ministry would never live up to its redemptive potential.*

So we launched a feedback system that would help candid conversations to occur. First, we agreed that those who received a grade of C on two consecutive occasions would see change in their future: either they would be relocated to a new ministry department, or they'd be asked to leave altogether. No reasonable employee with even moderate self-esteem wants to do C-level work on a continuous basis. And no effective manager wants to oversee C-level work forever. Cs must be dealt with, plain and simple.

Second, regarding the Bs, we agreed not only that they were the backbone of our staff, but also that we needed a *substantial* number of them on board just to keep the church afloat. People who do consistent B-level work are typically good performers with good attitudes. They may never offer up big, breakthrough ideas, but their steadiness and faithfulness are essential assets to any organization.

Finally, regarding the "A" contributors, we acknowledged that even the best organizations have a relatively small percentage of them, and no organization can have too many. We unapologetically decided to feed them extra resources and extra learning opportunities. We decided to make sure they felt appreciated and challenged. "A" teammates are rare and deserve to be identified and celebrated.

I may be naive, but I believe that deep down, everyone in an organization wants to know if they are succeeding or failing. Our A-B-C approach is far from perfect, but to its credit, it is clear.

LINKS

#23 - FIRST TESTED [PG. 80]
#38 - REAL-TIME COACHING [PG. 115]
#41 - KEEP SHORT ACCOUNTS [PG. 123]
#59 - LET'S DEBRIEF [PG. 172]

41 | KEEP SHORT ACCOUNTS

When high-capacity people work in close proximity to each other, there will be friction. To expect otherwise is naive because inevitably something is going to be said or done by someone and someone else's feelings are going to get hurt.

What matters is what you do immediately after the infraction occurs. As far as I can tell, there are two theories in existence here. One says to let time heal the wound. Don't pay too much attention to the thing: the other person will forget about it, your own anger will subside, and eventually all will be water under the bridge.

And then there's the Bible's approach.

Ephesians 4:26 says never to let the sun go down while you are still angry. Matthew 5 teaches that if you are in a worship service and remember that you are holding ill will toward someone, you should excuse yourself and go try to reconcile that very hour. The more time that elapses between the infraction and the attempted resolution, Scripture implies, the more likely it is the rift will grow.

If you're like me, you can readily think of situations in which you've had a hurtful exchange with someone but, because of pace or pride, you decided to stick with the day's schedule and move on. But moving on becomes increasingly difficult because your mind is distracted by that conversation with your colleague that was anything but collegial.

Not that I've ever done it myself, of course, but I've heard tales of people stewing over these situations for days on end—months, even, or sometimes years. They stew so long that they begin thinking of the other person differently. More time passes, and they find themselves imagining schemes in which the other person is actually out to get them, as if executing some macabre plot. The day finally comes when the person is no longer a person but an "axis of evil" in human flesh.

I gave a sermon on this topic one time at Willow, and I had our producer roll a grill onto the stage as I began the message. The grill had a rotisserie on it. At a certain part in my talk, I walked over to the grill and said, "When you and another person suffer a relational breakdown and you don't address it immediately, it's like you stick them on a spit. You turn them over and over and over until the heat of your anger begins to burn. You continue to think of new reasons why he or she is such a terrible person, and before you know it, you grill that person into an unrecognizable version of who they once were. At this point, reconciliation is the furthest thing from your mind. Homicide, yes. Humbly forgiving them, no."

How much better it is to make a pact with the people around us that says, "Whenever an infraction occurs, let's commit to addressing it and resolving it as soon as possible. Both of us. Deal?"

I tell my direct reports and colleagues that if I say something to them in a meeting or in the hallway that later causes them to start turning me over in their mind like I'm on a spit, I'd like them to waste *no* time in calling me. I'd gladly step out of a meeting or get out of bed if it means reconciliation can happen fast.

Our senior leadership team had a very animated meeting recently. There were eight or nine of us in the room, as I recall, and some intense issues surfaced that elicited dynamic debate for the better part of two hours. When I dismissed the meeting, I felt good about where we had left things and even better about how invested everyone had been in the discussion. But thirty minutes later, my private line rang. "Bill, a lot was said in that meeting," my colleague started. "Are we okay?"

I told my teammate that while I genuinely appreciated his call, I hadn't given his comments a second thought. "We agreed to keep short accounts," I said. "If I'd felt stung by anything you said, I'd have been the one picking up the phone to dial. I'm great! Really, I am. But thanks for the call."

I've been on the other end of those calls on many occasions. I'd be in a flaming-hot meeting and would spout off with a heartfelt opinion, only to realize later that I'd overstepped a verbal boundary. I would start feeling guilty about what I said and would have to pick up the phone and call the offended party to say, "Hey, I'm feeling a little troubled about that last comment I made to you in the meeting. It landed a little more personally than I intended it to. I want to keep short accounts with you. Are we okay?"

The healthiest organizations I see are not conflict-free. They are just ridiculously committed to keeping short accounts.

Those are no-lose phone calls, my friend. If there hasn't been a violation, you've proven that you're a short-account person. And if there has been an infraction, you are addressing it before you are tempted to put them on the spit. The healthiest organizations I see are not conflict-free. They are just ridiculously committed to keeping short accounts.

#33 - JUST SAY IT! [PG. 104]
#59 - LET'S DEBRIEF [PG. 172]
#61 - ARE WE STILL HAVING FUN? [PG. 175]
#67 - ALWAYS TAKE THE HIGH ROAD
      [PG. 194]

42 | WE GOT TO DO THIS TOGETHER!

An exhilarating dynamic of leadership for me has always been overcoming big challenges in the context of a team. I love nothing more than to form an interdependent team, present a massive problem to its members, and then lead a process whereby we attempt to reach solutions. It may take a few hours or it may take a few years, but time is not the point. The point is assembling the players and melding them into a team that loves each other and reaches its goals together.

Over the years, one thing I've tried to practice with increasing frequency is celebrating those team-oriented values once we reach the end of our time together. Sometimes I'll draw everyone into a circle and say, "Gang, as thrilling as it was to solve the problem we solved, I want you to know that it was just as meaningful to me that we got to do it *together*."

The first time I uttered those words was on the heels of an international conference that felt as if it had been cursed. I'd flown an entire team overseas to help put on a several-day event, and every conceivable thing that could go wrong did. There were language complications, cultural complications, venue complications, technological complications, translation complications, transportation complications, and more. It felt as if we were in an alley fight for the better part of four days straight.

We had "fix-it" meetings in my hotel room until one or two in the morning and then had to head half-asleep to rehearsals three hours later. During breaks throughout the day, we'd huddle in the back room and figure out what adjustments we had to make after learning yet another wrench had gotten thrown into our plan. Finally, partway through the last session, there was an outpouring of the activity of God. It was amazing, but the tears it elicited could just as easily have been due to sheer exhaustion.

When the conference was finally over, I gathered everyone backstage and said, "This was one of the greatest kingdom fights I've ever been in. Thank you—each one of you—for fighting hard and for keeping watch over your attitude. It made all the difference in the world. By God's grace, we did it, gang. And we got to do it together."

The intensity of the fight made the victory that much more enjoyable, which was evidenced by the fact that I actually encouraged hand-holding around that little circle. I led a prayer with my team that day, thanking God for a shared memory we'll carry with us the rest of our lives.

After that, I took the "we got to do this together" statement with me into other large-scale kingdom fights. When we raised money for Willow's new facility, a core group of faithful Creekers helped me do the home meetings where we'd present the vision to small groups of people and ask them to consider making a pre-campaign pledge.

The intensity of the fight made the victory that much more enjoyable, which was evidenced by the fact that I actually encouraged hand-holding around that little circle. I led a prayer with my team that day, thanking God for a shared memory we'll carry with us the rest of our lives.

There were only five or six of us who served at all forty-two meetings, and after we dismissed the final crowd from my home, I gathered that small group together in my great room and commemorated their commitment. "Team, that was one of the steepest hills I've ever tried to climb at Willow, but we got to do it together. And as a result of our full engagement and God's full empowerment, we all wound up being better friends than we were before we went to battle!"

We enjoyed food and drinks and custom-made sweaters with a "42" embroidered on the front. To this day, whenever I see one of those teammates around Willow, I feel the same sense of camaraderie that platoon members must feel toward fellow fighters.

Next time you're in the midst of a kingdom fight, pray and fight hard, but at the end of the battle, make sure you honor the unique contribution of each individual who made the victory happen. They have to know that while you prioritize progress, you prioritize people even higher. They have to hear you convey the fact that even though you may never be in another great challenge together, this particular effort was unusually sweet. Try using the "we got to do this together" axiom. My prediction is that it will do everyone's heart good.

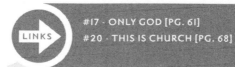

LINKS #17 · ONLY GOD [PG. 61]
#20 · THIS IS CHURCH [PG. 68]

teamwork and communication | 127

activity&
assessment

a blu

43 | A Blue-Sky Day

One of the most amazing gifts that God gives people is the ability to think creatively. So when things get stale at a church, it is a fair bet that God is not to blame. Usually it's that church leaders don't carve out the time, establish the right environment, and rally the requisite energy to think new thoughts.

Since the beginning days of Willow, creative teams I've led have always placed a high value on "blue-sky days" (or half-days, or hours). While the duration would vary, the meetings were always called for the sole purpose of dreaming. Periodically I'd gather the team, present an interesting challenge, and then ask them to remove every single boundary, restriction, and practical consideration from their brains. The question I encouraged them to consider was "What would we do to advance the kingdom of God if there was nothing to stop us from doing it?"

What if we had no family obligations, no job stresses, no time constraints, no budgetary or personnel or facility restrictions, and no fear of failure? What would we do then?

A "blue-sky day" connotes unlimited visibility and unlimited ceilings. To create an atmosphere where bold, unbounded idea generation can occur, we usually choose to hold our blue-sky days off-site. A church member's home, a nearby resort, a cabin on the lake — almost any location will work, as long as it contributes to free thinking and idea creation.

The question I encouraged them to consider was "What would we do to advance the kingdom of God if there was nothing to stop us from doing it?"

We also make sure we allot enough time to break out of our normal restrictive thought patterns and into new, unshackled ways of thinking. Ministry people are so well trained to spot roadblocks and "reasons why not" that it may take more time than you think to get your team to play by the new rules. At first they'll feel ridiculous offering up ideas that have obvious limitations or flaws. But usually, if you hang with the approach long enough and keep assuring the group that "every idea is a good idea," creative momentum will eventually build.

When Willow went to a two-service format on Saturday nights—one at five o'clock and one at seven—we were inadvertently forced into a time slot for the second service that restricted its long-term growth. Especially for families with young children, seven o'clock on a Saturday night was a terribly inconvenient time to come to church.

I pulled together the brightest staff minds I knew and said, "Here's the challenge: we've got to figure out a way to grow that second service. We're stuck with the start time, but other than that, dream big. Go."

The end result of our time together was a series of fantastic ideas. We decided to break from the format we used for the weekend's other three services. We'd provide an alternative style of worship and shrink the message from thirty-five minutes down to twenty. We'd tack on a fifteen-minute Q&A session and have open mics positioned throughout the congregation. We'd restrict pastors' answers to ninety seconds so they wouldn't be able to sermonize. And we'd project a giant countdown clock on both side screens so that attendees could help keep the pastors honest.

Eventually the format led to the creation of "My Story" segments, in which people share three-minute testimonies of how they came to faith and what their faith meant to them in their daily life, in hopes of inspiring others toward a God-centered life. Some of our best and freshest ideas came out of that blue-sky day.

We've also used blue-sky days for purposes other than problem eradication. Our creative team once held a blue-sky meeting to dream about "buzz" events. Our goal was to come up with half a dozen services that were completely different from our weekend fare, services that would catch our congregation a little off-guard and stimulate spiritual growth.

Most of the ideas generated that day were outrageous and unworkable. But some found a home on that year's schedule and absolutely blew Willow's minds. One weekend, for example, I hosted leaders representing four different faith traditions—Hinduism, Buddhism, Judaism, and Christianity—on the main stage. I stood in the center aisle with a microphone and invited them to explain what their religions taught about issues of morality, salvation, eternity, and who they thought Jesus Christ really was. The interest level of our congregation was through the roof, and I was humbled after every service to see just how many people were impacted by the distinctions they picked up that weekend.

Another time, we hosted country-music superstar Randy Travis in concert and invited him to share his faith story.

We did interviews with leaders who were giving their lives to ending global poverty and HIV/AIDS; we did thirty-minute resident-artist segments in which godly singers and painters and dancers would perform mini-concerts to set up the message for that weekend. And it all came out of that blue-sky exercise.

I have encouraged all the leaders at Willow to adopt a blue-sky practice of their own, regardless of whether they consider themselves "creative types." In my view, any group that is conducting any sort of ongoing activity runs the risk of operating from a rut over time. The easiest way to climb out is to be given permission to think completely differently than you have ever thought before. Finance departments that have been doing their accounting procedures the same way for two decades might need to blue-sky issues like how to track numbers more efficiently or how to structure themselves in a more innovative fashion. Senior leadership teams may need to blue-sky how to conduct their recurring meetings so that their best energies stay reserved for kingdom-building instead of feeding bureaucratic monsters.

In 2002, University of Southern California President Steve Sample wrote a book called *The Contrarian's Guide to Leadership*.[13] It so impacted me that I made it required reading for all of my senior staff. In the very first chapter, he writes about the power of "thinking gray and free" and explains the concept this way:

> The leader whose thinking is constrained within well-worn ruts, who is completely governed by his established passions and prejudices, who is incapable of thinking either gray or free, and who can't even appropriate the creative imagination and fresh ideas of those around him, is as anachronistic and ineffective as the dinosaur. He may by dint of circumstances remain in power, but his followers would almost certainly be better off without him.

Harsh words, perhaps, but ones I couldn't agree with more.

Grab your team and dream a little, leader! Ditch your restrictions and let the sky be your limit. The results might breathe new life into everyone!

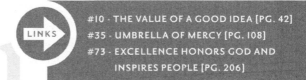

LINKS

#10 · THE VALUE OF A GOOD IDEA [PG. 42]
#35 · UMBRELLA OF MERCY [PG. 108]
#73 · EXCELLENCE HONORS GOD AND INSPIRES PEOPLE [PG. 206]

44 | THE BIAS TOWARD ACTION

USA Today ran a story one time about a guy who slipped into a coma on the heels of a terrible auto accident. He didn't stay there for nineteen days or even nineteen months, but rather for nineteen *years*. They interviewed him right after he awakened from all that unconsciousness and asked, "How is it that you finally were able to start talking?"

"Well," he said, pausing to consider it for the first time, "I just decided to start moving my lips."

As I read the newspaper article I couldn't help but think, "If all it took to break out of a nineteen-year coma was to start moving your lips, why didn't you give that a shot ten years ago? You might be giving public speeches by now!"

Personally, I've never understood inactivity. Why a person would sit when he could soar, spectate when he could play, or atrophy when he could develop is beyond me. I feel sure Jesus felt the same way. A lot of adjectives might describe Jesus' time here on planet Earth, but *comatose* would not be one of them. In the span of three years in "vocational" ministry, he performed dozens of miracles, healed hundreds of people, catalyzed thousands of conversions, set the stage for the most ambitious church plant in history, and died for the sins of all humankind. He was the epitome of action-orientation.

> *Personally, I've never understood inactivity. Why a person would sit when he could soar, spectate when he could play, or atrophy when he could develop is beyond me.*

What's more, he sought out followers who shared his bias toward action. Take the apostle Paul—talk about an activist! Jesus dramatically interrupted the man's rage-fueled trek to Damascus because he knew that once Paul's energies got channeled in a God-honoring direction, he would be a force of nature for the cause of Christianity.

And then there was Peter. Luke 5 says that one day Jesus was standing by a lake, preaching to a group of people. Needing a little distance from the swelling crowd, Jesus decided to continue his sermon from the water. He saw a couple of boats along the shore, left there by fishermen who were washing their nets, and so he hopped into one and asked its owner—Simon Peter—to row him out from shore. Once in the waves, he resumed his talk.

Certainly Jesus possessed the skills necessary to row himself out to sea. But taking matters into his own hands that way wouldn't have yielded any new information about the person he was thinking about drafting onto his team. Jesus wanted to find out what would happen to Peter when struggles or challenges came his way, and so he put Peter to the test.

"Give me a hand here, would you, Peter?" That was the request Jesus made. And without so much as a second thought, Peter said yes. Of course I'll help. Of course I'll spring to action when a need arises that I can help meet. Absolutely, yes!

More important even than the apostle's yes, though, was the motivation behind it. Peter's yes oozed out of his wiring, not out of obligation. He didn't know he was being tested. All he knew was that a need had presented itself that he was perfectly equipped to meet. And so he met it.

Because of his solid bias toward action, Peter passed the test, Jesus finished the sermon, and kingdom gains were netted.

The whole thing seems so simple, so elementary, but be honest: do *you* screen for action-orientation when you want someone to join you near the center of your cause? Are you intentional about seeking out the ones who by virtue of sheer wiring patterns will say, "Your dilemma is my dilemma too"?

Think about this with me: had Peter responded to Christ's request with moaning and groaning about how he'd been up all night ("Come on, Jesus, can't you see I'm *exhausted*?") or how he had so many other things to tend to ("Can't you find someone else to tend to such a menial task?"), he might have missed his whole kingdom adventure. Jesus was looking for an action guy because he knew how much energy his cause would take. And if he recruited action-oriented people in his day, then what does he expect from us, his current cadre of leaders?

If there's a downside to having a bias toward action and surrounding yourself with activist types, it's that they can get a little wound up at times. Even the apostle Peter found himself in a state of hyperactivity one time, and right in front of Jesus. Remember when Peter whacked off a guy's ear just before Jesus was arrested and taken away? Jesus healed the poor man and probably even gave him upgraded hearing before chastising Peter for his error. But I have to wonder how upset Jesus really was. I'd rather rein in a hyperactivist once in a while than have to wake him up from a long after-noon nap. And of this I am certain: what we are trying to build—the local church, the hope of the world—will not get built by hammock-swinging, pipe-smoking, video-watching, sleepy types. It just won't. It's way too tough a task!

I coach pastors all over the world in the belief that God is still looking for people who will roll up their sleeves and shovel something—anything!—rather than lean on the shovel's handle, pontificating about the horrible state of affairs in the world.

I was helping a Willow Creek Association church with a building initia-tive a few years ago, and en route from the airport to the church, the senior pastor and I talked about this "bias toward action" concept. He told me that whenever he's considering hiring someone new, he gives the person a driving test. Are they looking for the fastest lane? The shortest route? An edge on nearby drivers?

We happened to be sitting at a stoplight while he was telling me all of this, and somewhere midparagraph, the light changed from red to green. I waited a few seconds for him to notice, but no such luck. Finally, I couldn't choke it back: "It's as green as it's gonna get, Mario. If you're so action-oriented, then step on it! I'm dying here!"

Friend, it's as green as it's gonna get in our world. The doors are open, the path is clear, the harvest is huge, and the time to act is now. I believe God is looking to pour out his favor on those who are hopping out of bed each morning ready to further the cause for his glory. *Lead* with a bias toward action. Surround yourself with *others* who have a bias toward action. You will never regret it.

LINKS

#8 – HIRE TENS [PG. 38]
#23 - FIRST TESTED [PG. 80]

45 | Performance Buys Freedom

Aside from capital campaigns and new-building programs, a church's single largest expense is usually its personnel. So, as the guy in charge of stewarding salaries, positions, and people-resources, it has always been a top priority of mine to optimize our staff members to their fullest potential. But what does it mean to *optimize* them? For years I wondered how closely I should lead our staff, how tightly I should manage people. After lots of experimentation, here is where I have landed.

If staff members are doing their jobs really well—meeting or exceeding my expectations—then I give them more freedom and look over their shoulders less. I explain my spirit of liberty to them by saying, "You've earned this latitude with solid performance. Your diligence and thoroughness and 'win' rate have bought the privilege of my looser management style."

But if performance begins to sag, the monitoring increases—quickly. And if it *continues* to sag, official probes are organized, special meetings are called, and we get to the root of the issue soon. But the point is, the choice is my staff's to make. My part of the deal is crystal clear: performance buys freedom.

If staff members are doing their jobs really well—meeting or exceeding my expectations—then I give them more freedom and look over their shoulders less.

This philosophy supports the need for leaders to lead by strategic plan, because when a team sees eye to eye on the metrics, the deadlines, and the deliverables that are going to dictate ministry activity, it becomes painfully obvious how to objectify all of this "freedom" business. Let's say one of my direct reports is operating according to the strategic plan we've agreed to and I start poking around in her business as if she were off track. Our agreed-upon objectives are being met, she's performing on par with my expectations, and there truly is no cause for concern. Yet still, I nose around. In that situation, she has every right to say, "Hey, don't you have bigger fish to fry? All due respect, Bill, but my performance is speaking for itself."

Likewise, if her trend lines are down and her early goals are not being met, it is fair play for me to hang around her office a bit more and ask a series of questions. She would expect me to do so.

You have to decide for yourself how tightly to manage your team, but whatever you do, please *make the decision*. Many leaders never crystallize their management philosophy, and so they default to one of two patterns, suffocating control or abdication. Neither will work well over the long haul.

Don't leave this issue to chance. The people we lead and the God we serve deserve far better than that.

LINKS

#23 - FIRST TESTED [PG. 80]
#60 - PAY NOW, PLAY LATER [PG. 174]

SWEAT THE SMALL STUFF

The consensus among far too many seasoned leaders is that they fly too high and run too fast to be expected to sweat the small stuff involved in leading their organization. What's worse, the longer they lead, the more lax they become, justifying their increasing carelessness with the declaration that they're only "big-picture" people . . . fifty-thousand-foot people.

That attitude does a disservice to everyone they lead.

My peers are often shocked to learn that I send out between fifteen and two dozen handwritten notes a week to follow up with people who have helped us at Willow. Or that I respond to my critics when they take time to write. Or that I provide input to my assistant on which flights will work best for a given trip or that I occasionally look over the seating charts at key dinners we are hosting at Willow. These things may seem trivial to some people, but the best leaders I know right-size the amount of small stuff required to do their job well and then tend to those things fastidiously. They return phone calls and acknowledge correspondence. They answer followers' questions clearly and in a timely manner. They keep a finger on the financial pulse of their organization. They keep the board updated regularly with brief informal emails. I'm not suggesting they take on things their administrative staff can and should do for them, but the things they need to sweat, they sweat. And as a result, they're considered reliable, responsible individuals.

Years ago I stood in front of Willow's entire staff and reminded them of the importance of sweating the small stuff. It was the mid-1990s, and our church was growing rapidly. We had attracted many new families, and following nearly every weekend service, I'd greet a long line of newcomers who were seeking ways to get involved with our church. "We love the church and are eager to start volunteering here," they'd say. "But when we called for information, nobody called us back."

> *The best leaders I know right-size the amount of small stuff required to do their job well and then tend to those things fastidiously.*

My heart would sink. "Really? Do you remember who you called?"

They'd give me the details, and each time I'd keep a mental note of the departments or staff members mentioned. Over the ensuing weeks, I tabulated the number of times I heard of our children's staff or small-groups folks or student ministry team dropping the ball on returning calls, and then I called a church-wide staff meeting.

"Gang," I said patiently, "God has chosen to entrust our church with more people, and if we want to steward these people well, then we have to be responsive to them. I'd like to ask that you get back to folks within twenty-four hours of their call, even if only to explain that you don't have a volunteer position available at the present time. Please return every phone call. Nobody likes to feel ignored, especially at a church."

The staff agreed that they could do better, so I figured the issue was resolved.

Weeks went by, and to my surprise, the negative reports continued. I'd greet long lines of people and learn that they too had called the church and were promised to be called back but weren't. So I called another staff meeting.

"Maybe I wasn't clear last time," I said. "What I intended to communicate was that I expect *each* person in this room to return *every single* phone call within twenty-four hours of its receipt. No exceptions. I fully expect the flow of congregational complaints to trickle down to nothing by this time next month. Deal?"

The staff agreed they could do better, so again, I figured the issue was resolved.

More weeks went by, and still more complaints came in.

Yet a third staff meeting on this topic.

"I'm obviously incapable of getting this message across to you," I said with far less patience this time. "Either that, or else you're utterly incapable of hearing it. I am going to say this one final time, and then I will take the kinds of actions none of you wants me to take. You *will* respond to inquiries from the congregation, or you will no longer be employed here. If I keep hearing that your ministry is not responding to phone calls, I will pull your entire department into my office, I'll have the names and addresses and phone numbers of every disappointed congregant in hand, and bad stuff will definitely go down."

By the looks on their faces, I could tell the staff was horrified. "You can't do that!" they were thinking. But I assured them that I could. And that

I would, unless they took me seriously on this issue. Thankfully the staff finally responded aggressively and no bad stuff went down.

Now, I'm not necessarily advocating threatening your staff with ultimatums. But I do believe there are times when you have to raise the pitch level to the point where the organization will be reminded that small stuff does, in fact, matter. No matter who you are. No matter how busy you are and how many people you lead.

#7 - AN OWNER OR A HIRELING [PG. 34]
#39 - JUST TO BE CLEAR [PG. 117]
#70 - ARRIVE EARLY OR NOT AT ALL
[PG. 200]

47 | DOABLE HARD VERSUS DESTRUCTIVE HARD

Certain leadership axioms have come to me almost overnight. I'd experience a set of circumstances, formulate a clear point of view on the matter, and apply my newfound logic to my go-forward plan immediately.

This is not one of those axioms.

Those who know me well know that I'm intense and activistic. For me, the bigger the challenge, the more I like it. I've always pushed myself hard to solve problems, raise the bar, and make as many gains for God as I possibly can. But as the years rolled on, I found myself beginning to ask questions that I never asked as a younger leader. Questions like, Should growing a church be this hard? Should hiring staff be this hard? Should raising money and putting together messages and discipling people in their walks with Christ be this hard? Should the sum total of ministry life be *this unbelievably hard*?

The answer, I discovered, was yes. And no.

A quick read of Ephesians 6 says that we're in a struggle against rulers and authorities, against powers of this dark world.[14] I don't know about you, but to me that imagery would seem to say that yeah, ministry *should* be this hard. It's a raging battle against powerful forces!

But then you back up nine books and read Jesus' words: "My yoke is easy and my burden is light."[15]

So which is it?

I gathered my senior leadership team one day and told them I wanted to talk about whether the work we were doing was too hard. Interestingly, when you call a meeting to discuss how hard everybody's working, everybody shows up.

I asked them to describe the most difficult challenges they were presently facing, and I listened carefully to how they answered. Some admitted that the challenges faced by their particular ministry departments were the toughest they'd ever known. But as they talked about their stressors, their energy actually increased, their eyes brightened, and their posture seemed to straighten a bit. They'd use language like, "This is exhilarating!" "It's hard, but it's fun!" "We're praying our best prayers these days, and when we get to the top of this hill, we're really going to celebrate!"

"Okay," I thought, "so that's one kind of 'hard'—the fun and catalytic and inspirational kind of hard."

As we continued around the table, I noticed that other team members described their seasons of challenge using far different language. They talked about how they were losing sleep at night. They were experiencing anxiety and increased bouts of fear and despondency. They were having escapist thoughts. They were worried that they'd lose their jobs if they didn't set new excellence records with the various projects they were overseeing.

This was "hard" of another kind. It was *too* hard.

I walked over to a flip chart and asked if it would be profitable for us to think about ministry work in two distinct ways: "doable hard" versus "destructive hard." Heads started nodding in affirmation. I jotted the terms at the top of two columns and underscored the fact that some things in ministry are understandably hard. "If you're helping disciple someone who lived a self-destructive life before coming to faith in Christ," I said, "then you've really got your work cut out for you. It's hard work, bringing someone up the spiritual learning curve, but if it breathes life into you and raises your spirit to do that kind of work, then we'd probably all agree it should fall over here on the Doable Hard side of the equation."

They all agreed, so I kept going. "Likewise," I said, "if you have to put together five new sermons in a week and know that there are not enough available hours in that week for you to be able to prepare well, is it possible we'd all say that task is *destructively* hard?"

We continued citing examples of what constituted Doable Hard and what crossed the line into Destructive Hard and then made two agreements with each other. The first agreement was that we all needed to have the courage and determination to operate consistently in the Doable Hard category. If we wanted an easy profession, we said, then we should probably find something besides ministry to do.

The second agreement we made was that whenever we saw our approach to ministry bleeding over into the Destructive Hard column, we'd raise the flag of concern and talk with one another about how to shift expectations or change roles or alter assignments so that we didn't knowingly operate in a manner that would damage our souls, our bodies, our marriages, and our ability to minister effectively over the long haul.

I eventually talked to the entire staff about these ideas, and to this day, if someone comes into my office exhausted from a ministry hill they're climbing, we have the "doable hard versus destructive hard" discussion. It's the simplest way I know to keep ministry sane.

Years ago, psychologist Mihaly Csikszentmihalyi wrote a book titled *Flow* that explores what makes experiences genuinely satisfying. He discovered that when people felt strongest, most alert, most effortlessly in control, most unself-conscious, and at the peak of their abilities, it was because they had set challenges for themselves that were neither too difficult nor too simple for their abilities. "With such goals," he says, "we learn to order the information that enters our consciousness and thereby improve the quality of our lives."[16]

I can vouch for what this Hungarian author says because the last time I went through a "destructively hard" ministry era, I was a walking, talking antithesis of everything he describes—so much so that I came home one day, got out my journal, and wrote down these words:

Whenever we saw our approach to ministry bleeding over into the Destructive Hard column, we'd raise the flag of concern and talk with one another about how to shift expectations or change roles or alter assignments so that we didn't knowingly operate in a manner that would damage our souls, our bodies, our marriages, and our ability to minister effectively over the long haul.

> The way I am doing the work of God is destroying God's work in me. Something has to change. Soon.

We will surely face tough seasons in ministry. But if you ever find yourself consistently dreading your days, consistently feeling overwhelmed, and consistently dreaming of getting away (perhaps never to return), then your ministry pace and your ministry approach are probably killing what God hopes to accomplish in and through you. Get out a sheet of paper, draw your own columns, and right-size your challenge rate. Let's covenant together to keep ministry life sane.

LINKS

#49 - IS IT SUSTAINABLE? [PG. 147]
#73 - EXCELLENCE HONORS GOD AND INSPIRES PEOPLE [PG. 206]
#76 - FINISH WELL [PG. 214]

48 | DEVELOP A MOLE SYSTEM

Management schools often teach that responsible leaders stay within the chain of command when it comes to obtaining information about what's going on deep in their organization. In other words, the only people you're supposed to talk to are those who report directly to you. Both in my business career and throughout thirty-plus years of ministry, I have violated this instruction ... on purpose.

I believe that a responsible leader must rely on *many* channels of input to ascertain what is really going on in his or her organization. Consequently, through the years I've worked hard to find trusted individuals who love God, love the church, love me, and are courageous enough to tell me the truth, even when it's tough to hear.

These days I probably have dozens of communication conduits who provide candid, accurate insights regarding the various organizations I serve. With some of them, I strike an intentional arrangement wherein they provide me regular feedback on weekend services or conference sessions or how we are really doing in a department we have recently reorganized. With others, the approach is much more conversational and casual. But with all these folks—whether they know they're operating as my "moles" or not—the lines of communication are wide open.

Sometimes I query these folks for their opinions on various matters going on deep within the organization. Other times, I just make sure I'm available to receive any unsolicited information they care to convey. I don't necessarily act on every perspective I hear, but I find if I load my brain with lots of data, I'm better able to corroborate what my formal communication structures are telling me.

Most of the time, my informal channels simply support what my direct reports are telling me. But other times the word on the street doesn't exactly jibe with the assurances of one of my teammates. When this happens, I'll pull the person aside, probe their perceptions, and begin mulling over what I should do with that information.

My direct reports need to know that I have other sources than the ones sitting right in front of me week in and week out. If they're working hard and keeping me informed along the way, then the conversations I have when I get stopped in the parking lot or in a local restaurant or via my private email account should be of no concern. And if they have been painting a rosier picture than the truth, I don't mind their knowing that I'm likely to find that out over time.

> *My direct reports need to know that I have other sources than the ones sitting right in front of me week in and week out.*

LINKS

#25 - NO ELEVENTH-HOUR SURPRISES PLEASE [PG. 86]
#41 - KEEP SHORT ACCOUNTS [PG. 123]
#52 - FACTS ARE YOUR FRIENDS [PG. 155]

sust

49 | Is It Sustainable?

On an icy winter afternoon like only Chicago can muster, I headed to the nearby YMCA to do my run indoors. My plan was for thirty laps, and at about lap ten, I noticed another guy step onto the track and sprint as if he were competing for the hundred-yard dash. He ran fast and he ran hard, but six laps in, he ran flat out of steam.

As I passed the guy lying there, gasping for air, I thought, "You know, that looks an awful lot like me in my early days of leadership."

When I started out in church work, I was overly enthralled with any chart that was going up and to the right. It didn't matter how much energy I had to expend or how many resources *anybody* had to invest to continue that growth. As long as lives were being changed and the electricity bill was covered, I was content. I would thank God for the success we were seeing, never once realizing that our short-term gains were coming at an unrealistic price and pace for our staff and volunteers. The wins we were netting would be impossible to sustain.

Surely I'm not the only leader with a hard head about this issue of sustainability. Actually, I know I'm not, given how many pastors boast to me about how many ministries they launch every year, secretly hoping I will not ask how many of them crashed and burned six months later.

Personally, I don't want to launch something unless I have a strong sense that we can build it, resource it, and sustain it over the long haul. Good leaders call out high commitments from people. They cast pulse-racing visions and say, "If we all rally together, we can take this hill!" But at some point along the way, they have to ask themselves how many hills they realistically can ask their congregations to climb in a given time frame. And how many can their people actually sustain? Fail to think through the issues and you'll fry your church *and* yourself. And that's not a whole lot of fun for anybody.

When I first got involved in church work, my filter for determining ministry activity had only two criteria. As long as it advanced the kingdom and as long as we could effectively launch it, then "it" generally got approved. But over time, when our leadership team presented some new initiative they were all fired up about, I started adding a third consideration: *Is it sustainable?*

If the answer was no, we might tinker with the plan to see if we could make it so, but if we couldn't, we wouldn't launch. Crashes can sometimes cause terrible damage, both to the organization and to its people. Hearts get broken, and faith gets shaken. How much better to ask all three questions: Is it kingdom-advancing? Can we launch it well? Is it *sustainable?*

This idea hit home for me when Willow started its Latin American partnerships. The first year of our involvement, we invested a little over a hundred thousand dollars. The following year, we invested two hundred thousand. The year after that, three. You see where this is going.

Good leaders call out high commitments from people. They cast pulse-racing visions and say, "If we all rally together, we can take this hill!" But at some point along the way, they have to ask themselves how many hills they realistically can ask their congregations to climb in a given time frame.

By our eighth year, we were investing nearly a million dollars a year in this effort, sending almost a thousand volunteers to places like the Dominican Republic and Costa Rica on an annual basis. The partnerships were blossoming, and the net result of our involvement would likely yield freshly redeemed saints by the thousands. But I woke up one day and realized that at this rate we were soon going to be flying 747s full of Willow Creek folks down there and pouring our entire annual budget into this effort. Was it worthwhile? Absolutely. But could we sustain it? That was a far different question.

Our budget for Latin America had to crest somewhere. So I pulled together a meeting with our partners from that corner of the world and posed the one question nobody wanted to hear: "Instead of asking whether or not we can *start* effective partnerships with people in Latin America, I think we have to ask, Can we sustain them over the ten to twenty years to come?"

The discussion that ensued was a healthy one as we sorted through what level of volunteer involvement and ministry resource investment we were prepared to make—and make over the long haul. In the end, God led us to a support level that was both generous and sustainable.

It took a little time to adjust to this funding level, but our leaders eventually wound up turning something entrepreneurial into something *sustainable*. We recently celebrated twenty years of ministry in Latin America. I was very proud of our team.

The sustainability concept is catching on in kingdom circles, and its arrival is long overdue. As leaders of the most important endeavor on planet Earth, we have to get better about implementing what we can sustain. The people we partner with deserve it.

LINKS #3 -YOU'RE ALWAYS IN A SEASON [PG. 24]
#6 - BOLD MOVE [PG. 32]

activity and assessment | 149

50 | Don't Screw Up

Before you assume from the title of this axiom that I discourage my followers from taking risks, allow me to explain. When a leader creates a risk-tolerant environment where contributors are consistently encouraged to go out on a ledge and try something new, that leader tends to attract like-minded risk-takers to his or her camp.

Especially with eager, younger staff, the adrenaline rush of being entrusted with the keys to the kingdom car causes some people's enthusiasm to outpace their discernment. Sometimes I can almost see the bravado on their faces as they prepare to do a solo skydive for Jesus.

Along the way, I developed a shorthand slogan to help with this exact situation. I'd look straight into those confident young eyes and say, "This really is a thrilling opportunity you are being entrusted with, and I'm happy for you! But can I give you a piece of advice? Don't lose your better judgment in the elation of launching something new. Think things through. Cover the details. Do the requisite follow-up so that you increase the likelihood that this fun new kingdom thing will actually work over the long haul." And then, with just enough of a smile to confuse them, I'd add, "Don't screw up."

It's common language around Willow now. Someone will ask my permission to get a new initiative off the ground, and before I can get a word in, they'll say, "Now, I know you're going to tell me not to screw up, and so I want you to know that I am *not* going to screw up. I'm going to tend to every detail and make sure we launch it right."

"I'll hold you to that!" I say.

> *Especially with eager, younger staff, the adrenaline rush of being entrusted with the keys to the kingdom car causes some people's enthusiasm to outpace their discernment. Sometimes I can almost see the bravado on their faces as they prepare to do a solo skydive for Jesus.*

When you think about it, leaders build credibility by not screwing up. If you keep fumbling kingdom opportunities, who is going to offer you the next opportunity?

Jesus taught that if you're going to go to battle, you'd better get a troop count and know precisely what you're up against. If you're going to build a building, he also advised, know your budget and stick to it or you'll never get it built.

In essence, I'm saying the same thing: "I hope you have a boatload of fun with this exciting initiative and help a ton of people while you're at it. But keep your head about you every step of the way. Know your plan. Test your assumptions. Manage your resources. By doing so, you will earn the trust and the privilege of doing much more in the future."

LINKS

#12 - TAKE A FLYER [PG. 49]
#54 - EVERY SOLDIER DESERVES
        COMPETENT COMMAND [PG. 161]
#57 - DID WE DO ANY LEARNING? [PG. 168]

51 | SOSs

When our staff was small and I didn't yet have a secretary, people would come in and out of my office all through the day to keep me apprised of the goings-on in the organization. Occasionally someone would drop in and say, "Hey, Bill, were you aware that something has gone way wrong in the student group [or the music ministry or the singles ministry or in children's]?" I'd check it out, and quite often the tip I had received was not only accurate but it was understated. Something dishonoring or dangerous was going on, and I'd need to do my best to rectify the situation.

But once our staff numbered more than seventy-five, I had to accept the fact that I was no longer going to hear about all the issues that were going on deep in the organization. That was a bit unnerving to me.

So I pulled the staff together and told them I needed their assistance. "Whenever you spot something amiss around here," I said, "something that violates our values or something unhealthy or dangerous, I hereby give you permission to take the issue to your direct supervisor for immediate resolution. Consider yourselves empowered!"

Time passed, and this new process seemed to be going well. But then I noticed a trend. With increasing regularity, I'd walk the hallways as I went from one meeting to another and get stopped by staffers who weren't too thrilled with the new process. These were folks who at one time had been able to drop into my office whenever they wanted, but these days, I wasn't quite so easy to access. They'd start our conversation by saying, "Bill, *if you only knew* what was going on around here...."

I'd ask them to describe their concerns to me, and quite often, I'd get an earful.

After listening to each story, I'd ask why these issues weren't being resolved. My colleagues would look at me with wide eyes and say, "I took it to my supervisor just like you said, but he won't do anything about it! He doesn't think this is a big deal!"

After enough of these conversations, I realized I no longer had a guarantee that our collective team was committed to solving some of our serious organizational problems. I called another staff meeting, stood in front of the entire group that was now more than two hundred strong, and said, "Gang, new policy. If you see something that is dangerous, dysfunctional, or damaging to our values as you understand them, I am still asking you to take the issue to your direct supervisor. But if that person *doesn't act* on the issue in a reasonable amount of time, I want you to send me an SOS. You can send it by voicemail, email, snail mail, smoke signal, or Morse code. You can plant yourself by my car and wait for me in the parking lot or call me at home, I don't care. What I care about is that you find a way to get word to me when serious issues are going unaddressed."

"New policy. If you see something that is dangerous, dysfunctional, or damaging to our values as you understand them, I am still asking you to take the issue to your direct supervisor. But if that person doesn't act on the issue in a reasonable amount of time, I want you to send me an SOS. You can send it by voicemail, email, snail mail, smoke signal, or Morse code. You can plant yourself by my car and wait for me in the parking lot or call me at home, I don't care. What I care about is that you find a way to get word to me when serious issues are going unaddressed."

I told them that day that they had my full commitment to sending a reply to every SOS I received within twenty-four hours of its arrival. "Wherever I am in the world, and regardless of whether it's midafternoon or the middle of the night, if you send me an SOS, I will do my best to get back to you within twenty-four hours. Either I will act on it myself, I will commission an emissary, or I will tell you that while I appreciate your concern, the issue is not serious enough in my judgment to act on immediately. But you will hear back from me within twenty-four hours, one way or the other."

The SOS code became a very useful tool by which people who were deep in the organization could air their frustrations and assist in troubleshooting broken parts of our ministry. Some of the SOSs I received saved us from certain peril, such as when I found out that several of our maintenance volunteers had been hauling members of our grounds team from one part of our property to another in the front bucket of an end-loader. If someone had been hurt during one such joyride, well, you know ...

Others weren't quite so dramatic. One SOS alerted me to the fact that we had neglected to change the signage on a building we had just remodeled.

As a result, large numbers of people were getting lost en route from one part of our campus to another. As you'd guess, I asked if he had taken the issue to his supervisor. "Yes," he said, "but he said it's not in our budget to pay for new signs."

My nuttiness-meter sufficiently tripped, I told him I'd get right on it. I called the staff member's supervisor and asked how much new signs would set us back. He gave me the figure, and I said, "Listen, I'll raise the money myself if I have to, but we're not going to continue to point scores of people in the wrong direction just because we can't find a few hundred dollars to fix signs."

I've been told by CEOs of very large organizations that they often establish private email accounts and private phone lines so that the unsolvable problems of the organization can make their way to them. Good leaders chase out 95 percent of their organization's nuttiness by establishing clear vision statements, strong values, solid goals, and thoughtful policies. But they are never satisfied until that last 5 percent is shown the door. You have to sort out the system that's right for you. Around Willow, it has been the SOS approach. And thankfully, to my recollection at least, in twenty-plus years of relying on this approach, I have never once violated that magical twenty-four-hour rule.

LINKS

#25 - NO ELEVENTH-HOUR SURPRISES, PLEASE [PG. 86]
#29 - SPEED OF THE LEADER, SPEED OF THE TEAM [PG. 94]
#36 - HELP ME UNDERSTAND [PG. 110]
#41 - KEEP SHORT ACCOUNTS [PG. 123]
#52 - FACTS ARE YOUR FRIENDS [PG. 155]

52 | FACTS ARE YOUR FRIENDS

Perhaps in no other industry are facts more irrelevant to leaders than in church work. If you line up a hundred pastors whose churches are slowly dying and ask them how things are going at the church, you'll hear maddening things like, "We have a lot of people who are still very faithful," or "There's still quite a good spirit among those who remain," or "God's people have faced tough stuff like this since the beginning of time," or "Many of us believe our best days really are ahead," or "Sometimes you just have to hang on through eras like this, you know?"

I sometimes ask a question in response: "Do you know *why* things are in such a state of decline?" The answers I get make me shake my head in disbelief.

"Well, a new bar just opened down the road, and it seems there's now a demonic spirit of oppression infiltrating the whole community."

Or "Times have changed, Bill. I preach the truth, but no one wants to hear it anymore."

I could go on, but I think you get the point. These leaders give me any number of unverifiable ideas about why things are going badly for their church, but deep down, they don't really know.

"Have you ever thought about asking your people what's going on?" I ask. A blank look often surfaces at this point in the conversation, so I keep going. "I mean, what if you gathered a group of key people and actually probed the issues behind the church's decline from eight hundred attenders to five hundred to three hundred to a hundred and seventy-five? I think there are probably *very real* reasons why your ministry has been struggling, and I just bet they have very little to do with the new bar down the street."

Very seldom have I heard the response, "What a great idea, Bill! I'm going to get some of our folks together and have a few honest conversations." Far from it. What I usually get is "Thanks, but we're just going to pray our way through this. I know what the problem is—it's that demonic spirit of oppression I mentioned. And that bar ..."

Pretty frustrating.

I have come to the conclusion that some pastors whose churches are dying don't want to know the objective facts of their situation because they are genuinely afraid the raw information will be more than their hearts could bear. Imagine if the "facts" revealed that *they* were part of the problem, that *their* preaching or lack of leadership was contributing to the steady state of decline. Regardless, for far too many fear-stricken leaders, facts are not their friends. They would rather watch their church close its doors for good than to face the real problems and take responsibility for fixing what is broken.

Some pastors whose churches are dying don't want to know the objective facts of their situation because they are genuinely afraid the raw information will be more than their hearts could bear.

Many years ago, a pastor asked me to come do a consulting day with his staff. He hoped that I could come in and encourage his team a little so that their future would be brighter than their present.

I told the staff I wanted to break the day into two parts: during the morning hours, we would evaluate four key areas that can help define the success of many local churches—evangelism, discipleship, student ministry, and compassion initiatives—and then we'd spend the afternoon brainstorming ways to increase the effectiveness of each.

"I'd like you to break up into small groups," I explained, "and figure out how you'd rate your church's current effectiveness in each area. On a scale of one to ten—one being really bad, and ten being really, really good—assess how well you reach people far from God, help new believers grow up in Christ, inspire the next generation toward faith, and help solve the problems of our broken world. Come up with one number per group, and then come post your numbers on this flip chart. Deal?"

The staff members went right to work. Opinions bounced back and forth among the members at each table, and as time went by, everyone's energy for the exercise grew. They seemed genuinely honored to be asked for their input regarding how the church was doing and how it could get better.

Once all of the groups had posted their figures, I debriefed with the entire staff. Evangelism received fours and fives. Discipleship got mostly sixes and one seven. Student ministry ranked low—all threes. And compassion was at the very bottom of the heap. I made a few remarks and reminded everyone that after we took our lunch break, we'd hit the ground running on the solution side of things. "I've reserved the fun part for this afternoon," I said. "We're going to brainstorm innovative and inspiring ways to raise *every single* number at least two points in the next six months. Only positive ideas will be accepted, so come with your work gloves on. We'll cull the best thinking, pray over our work, and then call it a day."

I dismissed the group to a heartfelt round of applause. They were just as invested in and excited about the process as the groups at Willow who had been through the very same exercise four times a year for many, many years. In the quiet of my own heart, I thanked God for allowing the meeting to go so well.

Or so I thought.

The pastor who had sat silently all morning asked me if we could go for a walk. Once outside, he dropped a five-word bomb on me: "You can go home now," he said.

I stopped walking and caught his eyes. "Come again?"

"You can go home now, Bill. I have never been more humiliated in my entire life than I was this morning. Can you imagine what it felt like for me to sit at the back of the room and watch my entire staff criticize our ministry?"

I was floored. "But their assessments are *honest.* . . ."

He shot back, saying that until those negative assessments got aired, his staff was perfectly happy. "Now they think we have problems," he said. "And now I'm going to be walking around with a target on my forehead! They're going to blame *me* for all of this!"

I tried to explain that the *staff* wanted to take responsibility for resolving the issues they had raised, that they were *glad* the problems had been objectified so they could get busy finding solutions, and that the only role he had to play for now was to be a kind of choir director for all the new plans. But he wasn't exactly in the mood for my clarifications. Or my choir director analogy.

He had made up his mind, and in case I missed it the first two times, he looked at me and said, "You can go home now."

I drove away from that half day of consulting thinking about how for this particular pastor, facts were definitely not friends. He would have preferred that everything stay mushy and ill defined so that at the end of the day, no one would know the truth.

Maybe you can relate to the dynamic. Maybe facts haven't been your friends because you too were afraid of what they would reveal. Can I give you a loving piece of advice? Start warming up to facts. Eventually you'll come to the realization that when you have clear, objectified data, you can plan better, you can make better decisions, and you can chart a surer course for your church. Rather than cowering in fear, you'll find yourself confidently probing the congregation and staff and board members and volunteers in search of the facts—facts that finally are your friends.

LINKS

#7 - AN OWNER OR A HIRELING [PG. 34]
#46 - SWEAT THE SMALL STUFF [PG. 139]
#53 - FIND THE CRITIC'S KERNEL OF TRUTH [PG. 159]
#59 - LET'S DEBRIEF [PG. 172]

53 | FIND THE CRITIC'S KERNEL OF TRUTH

Emotionally healthy people don't particularly enjoy the attacks of a critic. But I must say, stinging words stung a whole lot more in my early days of leadership than they do today. Somewhere along the way, I conceded the point that the more influence you carry, the bigger the target you wear. And somewhere along the way, I got some really good advice.

A very wise man once told me that tucked deep inside every critic's attack is usually at least a tiny kernel of truth. And rather than reflexively lashing back at a critic, he advised, I should spend my energy figuring out what it is. "If you can identify it," he said, "you're likely to grow from it instead of devolving into defensiveness. Keep insisting on learning from these kernels of truth, and there just might come a day when you find yourself having to absorb less criticism. You'll have kept learning to walk straighter, discern better, and operate wiser and thus will be attracting fewer bullets."

A very wise man once told me that tucked deep inside every critic's attack is usually at least a tiny kernel of truth. And rather than lashing back, he advised, I should spend my energy figuring out what it is.

I never forgot that coaching. Finding the critic's kernel of truth is a tough discipline to master, but it *can* be mastered. You really can read critical things about you or your organization in the morning's local paper and resist the temptation to call the editor. You really can learn to hold the emotional sting in abeyance long enough to ask yourself, "Where is the kernel of truth here?"

When negative press surfaces about Willow or about me, I often gather my key leaders in my office, distribute copies of the release, and ask for their help. "This obviously reflects poorly on our ministry, but perhaps there is something we can learn," I'll say. "We probably all agree we don't deserve all of what's written here, but is there any portion of it we deserve? Where is the kernel of truth?" The conversations that ensue are not always pain-free, but they always prove useful to our continued collective growth.

LINKS

#3 -YOU'RE ALWAYS IN A SEASON [PG. 24]
#57 - DID WE DO ANY LEARNING? [PG. 168]
#67 - ALWAYS TAKE THE HIGH ROAD [PG. 194]

54 | Every Soldier Deserves Competent Command

Tom Clancy is best known for his dramatic military novels, but several years ago he wrote a historical account on the art of warfare. *Into the Storm: A Study in Command* is a profile of General Fred Franks, a guy who on the exterior looks anything but the part of a war hero—short statured, mild mannered, slight of build.[17] But on the inside, General Franks is the epitome of competence and confidence.

You read this book and discover along the way that your mind and heart are being stretched to full capacity as you learn about the life-and-death nature of this thing called leadership.

You follow Franks early in his career as he leads his troops through fire-fights in the jungles of Vietnam.

You suffer with him as he steps on a land mine that blows off his foot and confines him to a VA hospital for an interminable recuperation process.

You hope with him as he petitions the U.S. Army to allow him to serve as one of the few amputee commanders in U.S. military history.

You strategize with him as he puts together the entire ground operation for the 1991 Gulf War, involving hundreds of thousands of troops and tens of thousands of tanks and other supply vehicles.

You pray with him throughout the long and restless night before the invasion.

You agonize with him as he visits the front lines and sees some U.S. soldiers being zipped up in body bags, others being carried away on blood-soaked stretchers.

You celebrate with him as he congratulates every soldier he can get an audience with as Desert Storm goes down in history as one of the greatest military victories in our nation's history.

Even though I am repulsed by violence, I studied Franks's philosophy of war and was awed by one aspect in particular: In the heat of battle, the *leader* must be in the center of the action. It is the leader who must feel the pressure first, hear the sounds first, smell the smells first, and sense the momentum of the way things are going long before anyone else. *Every soldier deserves such competent command.* That was the phrase that kept banging around in my brain as I read. *Every soldier deserves competent command.*

Air-conditioned officers' quarters are no place for a leader whose troops are under fire. "You gotta get in the fight," General Franks would say. "Commanders must be visible. They must be present in order to ignite the soldiers' resolve. They must provide a bottomless supply of courage for soldiers to feed on when their own supply begins to dry up."

Twenty years ago, leadership guru Peter Drucker taught me that a leader has to make sure that everyone in the organization is being supervised by someone who is visible, present, and courageous — someone who is unmistakably *in the fight.*

"In any well-performing department," Drucker would say, "it's usually 40 percent of the workers who are making it so." And I discovered for myself that if that 40 percent is not being well led, a state of helplessness sets in, which becomes a commentary on the quality of leadership in the entire organization. The high performers in that department will jump ship, and you'll come to the sobering conclusion that you should have arrested the weak leader's freefall months or years before. Make no mistake about it: The cost for *not* paying attention to the issue of competent command is exponentially higher than whatever the cost is for doing so.

I don't typically lean into military metaphors, but as I read Clancy's account, I realized the parallels to ministry leadership were undeniable. I could barely put the book down. Or restrain my heartbeat. I underlined sentences and dog-eared pages and took notes in my journal, all because of my grave concern for leaders who are engaged in a higher-stakes conflict than even military combat.

In 1 Peter 5:8, Peter says, "The Evil One is a predator, seeking those he can devour" (my paraphrase). And Jesus himself reminds his followers not to be overly concerned about those who can only kill or maim the human body. "But be *really* concerned," he'd essentially say, "about the One who imperils the souls of men and women in eternity."[18]

I read page after page of Clancy's book and thought to myself, "It's high time that leaders in the local church got crystal clear on the intensity of the battle we're in and on what it will take to win." We are engaged in a wild spiritual battle for the hearts and minds and souls of human beings. As tragic as it is to see soldiers' dead bodies being stuffed into black bags, the stakes of our battle are infinitely higher. Our effectiveness, or lack thereof, seals men's and women's eternities: for us, it's not just a life-or-death deal. In our leadership battles, the stakes are *eternal* life and *eternal* death, a reality that has always been present in kingdom warfare. Jesus knew it, the Scriptures preach it, and we must believe it.

God is the giver of the leadership gift, and he fully expects us to keep heading straight into the fight until such time as he changes our orders or takes us home. We are in the highest-stakes battle in existence on the broadest battlefield of engagement ever imagined. Those we lead within the faith deserve our most competent, confident efforts. And Christ's instruction to reach the rest demands them.

> *We are in the highest-stakes battle in existence on the broadest battlefield of engagement ever imagined. Those we lead within the faith deserve our most competent, confident efforts.*

LINKS

#7 - AN OWNER OR A HIRELING [PG. 34]
#65 - LEAD WITH ALL DILIGENCE [PG. 190]

55 | BRAIN BREAKS

World-class performance coach Jack Groppel says that it's wholly unconstructive to think of your workday in terms of an eight- or ten-hour marathon in which you just keep running at a constant speed. "It's all about *oscillating*—,"[19] says Jack, leveraging bursts of energy and then giving yourself a break from stressors when necessary. I think he is right.

Whenever I'm in high-intensity planning or problem-solving meetings, I notice that there is a span of time when we can stay focused, followed by a span of time when all at once our brains seem to turn to custard. Everyone in the room seems to sit back with glazed eyes, silently declaring that their concentration capability is officially spent. Typically it occurs at the sixty- or ninety-minute mark: our rapid and fruitful progress comes to a screeching halt, and ideas flow slower than peanut butter.

I came up with a term to cue my team to the dynamic we were experiencing, as well as to signal the need to inject a little life into the situation. When I call a "brain break," everyone knows what's coming: a fifteen-minute time-out. Fifteen minutes to stretch physically, breathe outside air, and let the mental turbines cool down.

For me, a brain break usually involves getting up from my chair, grabbing a PowerBar, and walking around. It doesn't much matter where I go. The key is that I change postures, change rooms, and suck some fresh air. After only ten or fifteen minutes, my blood is flowing, my energy is invigorated, and my brain is ready to roll. Often the break affords me new ideas, and I find I gain another seventy-five or ninety minutes of productive work time compared to what I would have yielded had I just hunkered down and cranked out as much productivity as robotically possible.

> *When I call a "brain break," everyone knows what's coming: a fifteen-minute time-out. Fifteen minutes to stretch physically, breathe outside air, and let the mental turbines cool down.*

Your mind works according to rhythms of concentration that are beyond your control. It is your responsibility to know how long your bursts of brain power will last and how to recover when you find yourself at the end of one of those cycles. Invest in the airplane flight it will take you to read Jack's book on the basics of physiology and energy management, my friend. And bid brain paralysis a long-overdue farewell.

LINKS

#56 - SPEED VERSUS SOUL [PG. 166]
#73 - EXCELLENCE HONORS GOD AND
INSPIRES PEOPLE [PG. 206]

56 | SPEED VERSUS SOUL

When leaders lead effectively, they tend to generate an increasing amount of velocity in their own lives and in the organizations they serve. They usually wind up adding more staff, raising more money, caring for more people, and championing more causes. Over time, their "speed line" keeps going up and to the right.

But in church work, there's more to leadership effectiveness than this. Because in direct proportion to organizational growth, "good" pastors are also expected to *grow their souls* (I am using the term *soul* to mean our relationship with God and with those closest to us). This can be a real challenge for a guy like me, who prefers a pace no slower than Mach 2.

Somewhere along the way, I realized that although my speed line was content to run fast and hard after year, my soul line just couldn't keep up. At a certain velocity, most speed-hungry leaders will run out of the wherewithal to lead well. At a certain velocity, the soul will simply dissipate.

> *At a certain velocity, the soul will simply dissipate.*

I finished speaking at a conference in Germany one time, and my translator offered to give me a ride back to the airport. For the first part of that car ride, we talked quietly about the most impactful moments of the conference. We were making our way through a residential part of town, and our conversation matched the relaxed, easy pace. But then we turned onto the autobahn.

I began to notice that the faster my friend drove, the less frequently we talked. When we reached 250 kilometers an hour, our dialogue died down altogether. Instead of continuing the soulish interaction we'd been enjoying, we found ourselves focused solely on dodging the other cars and avoiding a crash.

I think there's an important lesson for us here: leaders have to adjust their velocity, or they will spend the most impact-rich years of their lives going fast but feeling empty on the inside.

These days, when I sense that my speed and soul lines are out of sync, I ask a simple question of self-reflection: In the various areas of my life, am I "gaining soul" or losing it?

In my relationship with God, is my soul line going up, or is it going down? Do I feel more aware of God's presence, more confident of his work in and through my life, more inclined to exhibit the fruit of the Spirit, and more determined than ever to help grow his kingdom? How is it between God and me?

In my relationships with family and close friends, is my soul line rising or falling? Especially as it relates to my wife and kids and grandson, do I sense an increased focus on their lives and personal development, or am I too wrapped up in work to care?

There have been eras in my life when my soul line has taken a nosedive. I'm not proud of those times, and I never want to repeat them.

There are other times when I have arrested the freefall and committed myself afresh to spiritual growth. It's on the heels of those seasons that I know my soul is gaining altitude once again.

If your soul line is suffering, maybe it's time to humble yourself and slow your pace. Alter your job description, your meeting schedule, and your spiritual practices if it means reclaiming the soulishness you need. "Don't gain the whole world," Jesus once said, "and lose your soul."[20] It's a worthwhile caution to heed.

LINKS

#47 - DOABLE HARD VERSUS DESTRUCTIVE HARD [PG. 142]
#65 - LEAD WITH ALL DILIGENCE [PG. 190]
#76 - FINISH WELL [PG. 214]

57 | DID WE DO ANY LEARNING?

What does a leader do when an initiative he or she is leading fails? There are lots of options: self-flagellation, berating others, and blaming external factors, among the others you no doubt could add to the list.

In recent years, I have preferred asking a simple question instead: Did we do any learning?

A staffer walks into the leader's office after having failed at a responsibility he was given. Reflexively the leader wants the staff person to understand the amount of credibility that was forfeited by this failure, not to mention the kingdom dollars that were squandered. "One thing is for sure," the thinking goes, "there must be consequences!"

> *"Did we do any learning?" It's the best response to failure I know.*

"Did we do any learning?" the leader immediately asks.

The emotional dynamic of the exchange is altogether different. And the possibility of honest dialogue is opened up, dialogue that can actually lead to coaching moments and future growth.

"Did we do any learning?" It's the best response to failure I know.

LINKS

#15 - THE DANGERS OF INCREMENTALISM [PG. 56]
#53 - FIND THE CRITIC'S KERNEL OF TRUTH [PG. 159]

58 | Create Your Own Finish Lines

Ministry leaders are in the people business. And because people are perpetual works in progress, there is no end to the amount of work we could do to serve them better. There are always more appointments that could be taken, more follow-up calls that could be made, more handwritten notes that could be crafted, more encouragement that could be offered, and more prayers that could be prayed. Therein lies the challenge and the question: When is enough enough?

I spend a lot of time with fantastic leaders of local churches from almost every country around the globe, and sometimes, just to spike interest in the room, I'll ask how many of them know precisely when their workday is done, or when their work is "officially" over. Often they look at me incredulously and remind me that church work is never finished and that a ministry leader's job is never done. I nod in agreement just before reminding them that their sustainability demands a different approach.

Most long-term efficiency studies show that if you work more than ten hours a day, you begin to live in a diminishing-return dynamic, and your effectiveness and results will actually go down. I believe these studies.

I'm an early riser, so for me, a typical workday runs from six in the morning until four in the afternoon. By four o'clock, my meeting parade halts, my computer is shut down, and my assistant is bid a fond farewell. It's my day's finish line, and I protect it vigorously. I also assign a ritual to it so that I can celebrate it

> *There are always more appointments that could be taken, more follow-up calls that could be made, more handwritten notes that could be crafted, more encouragement that could be offered, and more prayers that could be prayed. Therein lies the challenge and the question: When is enough enough?*

fully, in this case, a three-mile run with my neighbor followed by a shower, some civilian clothing, and a heartfelt thanks to God for accepting my best efforts throughout a day that is now *over*.

Having a daily finish line means work stays at work when I head home. It means sermon prep gets slotted for the following day instead of trailing me through the front door of our house. It means that once I ease into nonleader mode, my wife and kids are not asked to vie for my time with my ministry cares and concerns.

Since I began talking about this finish-line philosophy, I've heard reports from all over the world of people who are beginning to adopt it. One that stuck with me was the story of a female executive pastor in New Zealand who suffered serial bouts with anxiety. She worked incredibly hard and was known for making great kingdom progress, but her pace was slowly wearing her down. After sitting in a mentoring session of mine, she decided to implement a daily finish line. The line was drawn at five o'clock, and the ritual she attached to it was to meet a friend of hers—a senior leader who held a corporate post—at a nearby coffee shop.

The two women would meet for thirty minutes to recap their day and celebrate whatever progress had been made. After adhering to this pattern for a few months, the executive pastor saw real improvements. She told me that by the time she hit her driveway after her coffee ritual each day, she felt like a totally different person. "I am a better wife to my husband, a better mom to my kids, and a better leader to my team, now that I have allowed myself to be human once more."

Create your own finish lines—daily and also weekly. The pages of Scripture encourage all believers to set aside a time of "nonwork" at the end of every week—a practice that is somewhat crazy-making to people involved in ministry. You devote yourself to moving the ball up field for five days straight, only to come to a weekend and realize you're expected to work really hard at all of the services. Ministry becomes nonstop over time, and resentment sets in. I know this because I fell into the seven-days-a-week pattern for fifteen years straight and consequently was ground down into a state of exhaustion that took years to recover from. One of my discoveries during that era was that I was not immune to needing a Sabbath. I had to have a weekly finish line. I think you do too.

These days, after I greet the last person in line at Guest Central following Willow's final service on Sunday, I consider my weekly finish line crossed. I head toward the doors and make the short trip from Chicago to

South Haven, and as I pull into the long gravel driveway of our tiny cottage on Lake Michigan, I exhale and thank God for a full week of his sustaining power and grace. When I reach the carport, I put the week behind me and am freed up to be a nonworking, nonleading person who has full permission to engage in a non-Willow life for the rest of Sunday and all day Monday.

The practice has been a ministry-saver for me in ways I probably never will understand.

In terms of a monthly finish line, I try to get alone with God and relish a little solitude at least once every thirty days. The time affords me unique opportunities to do intensive reading, intentional reflection, and a bit of personal evaluation. I also set aside a slice of time when I can be around people who can build into me and challenge me to lead at higher levels. Sometimes it's a leadership development conference. On other occasions, it's a stimulating roundtable discussion with a handful of leaders from the marketplace. For a ministry leader who is perpetually in "output" mode, input-oriented finish lines like these feel fantastic every month.

I'm also a firm believer in annual finish lines. One of the best decisions I ever made was to attach the symbolic ritual of Willow's summertime baptism service to my annual finish line. There's nothing better than capping off another ministry year with the baptizing of hundreds of freshly redeemed people and then getting in my car and cranking up the worship music as I drive off on my summer study break. The practice helps me to feel God's pleasure in ways I really can't put words to.

Finish lines allow us those moments of emotional completion. They help us hear God say, "Enough is enough." They remind us that we are more than leadership machines. If you've never created your own finish lines—and established the requisite rituals to accompany them—do it now. Daily, weekly, monthly, annually; you'll never regret it.

LINKS

#47 · DOABLE HARD VERSUS DESTRUCTIVE HARD [PG. 142]
#56 · SPEED VERSUS SOUL [PG. 166]

59 | LET'S DEBRIEF

Even world-class leaders who are leading at the top of their game have an incurable desire to get better. Great teachers want to teach even better, great vision-casters want to cast vision even better, great team-builders want to build even better teams. They want to do *everything* better because they know that when *continuous improvement* ceases to be upheld as a core value, excellence wanes, communication gets tangled, and vision gets fuzzy. Little mistakes accumulate and eventually rule the day.

Every time I see a ministry leader losing his or her developmental edge, I think, "Your negligence is going to bite you. You think it won't, but it will. You think you can drift into improvement, but you can't. It takes hard work to get better!" And one way to force continuous improvement is to practice the discipline of debriefing.

To "debrief" something simply means to evaluate it from top to bottom. It involves honestly assessing a recent activity or initiative and determining what went well, what didn't, and why. Debriefings are not about judgment and condemnation and ripping something to shreds; they are about taking responsibility for the good, the bad, and the ugly. They are about learning from each and every leadership play in hopes of improving play over the long haul.

> *Debriefings are not about judgment and condemnation and ripping something to shreds; they are about taking responsibility for the good, the bad, and the ugly.*

The most important conference we do at the WCA each year is the Leadership Summit. Tens of thousands of ministry and marketplace leaders gather at hundreds of venues all over the world to try to get better at leadership. After such a significant event, I believe it's absolutely critical to gather highly discerning leaders together and talk about what worked well and what didn't. So for many years now, ten days following the Summit, we convene scores of pastors for a day-and-a-half-long debriefing. We ask, "Was this session helpful? Why or why not? Did we deliver enough skill training? Enough inspiration? Was our challenge bar set high enough?"

A few months ago, we did one of these post-Summit debriefings in a downtown-Chicago hotel and had an absolute ball. It felt like a class reunion. The decibel level during the first evening's dinner was so high that by the end of the night, I could only hear what was being shouted directly into my ear from three inches away. The following day, the energy in the room only grew as we culled the best and brightest ideas from the entire group and dreamed about what next year's conference might hold.

Once again, I was overwhelmed by the plentiful and helpful feedback we received. Once again, I was humbled by the gracious, generous spirits of these busy, burdened leaders who stopped what they were doing, took time away from their congregations, and jumped on airplanes bound for O'Hare, just to help us get better.

I reflected on it later and came to the conclusion that most people really are more than happy to help make something better. But it won't happen unless they are asked to do so. Leaders must invite people to slow down, do the hard work of honest evaluation, and marshal their best thoughts and ideas for improvement if their organizations are ever going to get better on a continual basis.

True, the post-Summit debriefings require a significant investment on everyone's part, but you can't argue with the results. The Summit has gotten better every single year as a result of the commitment to debrief.

Rally the troops after your next initiative—a conference, a communion service, an evangelistic event, a board retreat, a weekly team meeting, whatever—and engage them in your own debriefing. I bet you'll benefit from what you learn.

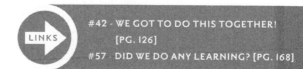

LINKS

#42 - WE GOT TO DO THIS TOGETHER! [PG. 126]

#57 - DID WE DO ANY LEARNING? [PG. 168]

activity and assessment | 173

60 | PAY NOW, PLAY LATER

High-capacity leaders know that to be successful in whatever endeavor they put their hands to, they must discipline themselves to do the critical tasks first. In construction, you've got to dig the hole and lay the foundation before the steel soars skyward and the windows are installed.

You have to pay before you play.

When I come into my office every day, I see scores of ways I can play. There are people who would love to play with me through email or on the phone or over a nice cup of coffee and a recreational chat. Even at this stage in my life and leadership, the temptation to play is so unbelievably high that I have to start my self-talk routine as I drive onto the campus: "Bill, when you walk through the door and sit down at your desk, these are the things you absolutely must get done. You'll feel so much better at the end of the day if you will forge ahead with these critical tasks and move them up field. You cannot play first, Bill. You first must pay."

High-capacity leaders know that to be successful in whatever endeavor they put their hands to, they must discipline themselves to do the critical tasks first.

And after a full day of "paying," I find that the "play" that follows is so much sweeter. Try it! I promise you'll like it.

LINKS

#29 - SPEED OF THE LEADER, SPEED OF THE TEAM [PG. 94]
#58 - CREATE YOUR OWN FINISH LINES [PG. 169]

61 | ARE WE STILL HAVING FUN?

Romans 8:6 says that the mind set on the flesh is death, but the mind set on the Spirit is *life and peace.* Life and peace—it's the kind of vitality and energy and enthusiasm that you feel well up in your soul and bubble over in ways that people on the outside can easily detect. It's undeniable when you're operating from a place of life and peace. Calmness and assurance and a sense of "fit" characterize your entire aura.

In leadership terms, we carry a responsibility to lead in such a way that those we lead are as freed up as possible to do their jobs from a place of life and peace. Are they slotted properly in terms of position? Are they carrying the right load? Are organizational expectations of them extremely clear? The shorthand way I stay apprised of this stuff is by asking my staff and colleagues, "Are we still having fun?"

Are we still having fun? I'm not asking if things are easy or if challenge spikes ever occur. I'm asking if there still exists something fundamentally life-giving about the role they're playing and the job they're doing. I'm a firm believer that if you're doing exactly what God is asking you do and are doing it in the right organization from the right seat within that organization, there ought to be an accompanying satisfaction and good pleasure about the whole deal. So when I ask the question and get an instant smile in return, I know we're on the right track. When I hear "Bill, I love what I do," I exhale.

> *In leadership terms, we carry a responsibility to lead in such a way that those we lead are as freed up as possible to do their jobs from a place of life and peace.*

But when I ask the question and they miss the one-count, I've already gotten my answer. If one of my colleagues can't answer whether we're still having fun quickly and definitively, red lights start flashing in my mind and I want to gently unpack what is depleting their fulfillment level.

I've been told that some leaders really don't care all that much about the "life and peace" factor of their cohorts. I'm not one of them. Someone's sense of job satisfaction and personal vitality means almost as much to me as the deliverables they're paid to achieve. If they are setting performance records but aren't having fun, we have a sustainability issue on our hands. (If they're *not* hitting it out of the park but are having a grand time, that's a problem as well, but at least they're adding to staff morale!)

When we are focused on the right mission and have the right people executing roles that are consistent with their gifts and calling, I expect to see a bounce in people's step, a sparkle in their eyes, joy in their hearts, and energy to spare.

Effective ministry leadership has a lot to do with keeping spirits buoyed and people uplifted so that they feel appreciated for going above and beyond what they would give in a typical job. I'm a firm believer that we're never going to end up with the most God-honoring results possible unless we're all still having fun along the way.

LINKS

#25 - NO ELEVENTH-HOUR SURPRISES, PLEASE [PG. 86]
#29 - SPEED OF THE LEADER, SPEED OF THE TEAM [PG. 94]
#41 - KEEP SHORT ACCOUNTS [PG. 123]
#52 - FACTS ARE YOUR FRIENDS [PG. 155]

NEVER BEAT THE SHEEP

Disappointments are frequent in the church-leading life. You launch a brand-new outreach campaign, thinking a certain number will participate, but only half sign up. You agree to help with a Habitat for Humanity home in your area but get to the job site and find only half the number of volunteers who promised to be there. You take a special year-end offering but still find yourself thousands short of goal.

So often in church work, expectations don't get met, goals don't get achieved, and results don't come in the way we think they should. And when that happens, an almost reflexive reaction tends to rise up in a leader's spirit: *I must beat the sheep!*

"Those terrible sheep!" the leader thinks. "If they had behaved properly, we would have maxed out the evangelistic event, built the house, and raised the funds. But no, they refused to cooperate, and now look where we are!"

You think of the days when shepherds carried around big sticks and could just smack their sheep when they didn't do what they were supposed to do. "*Bad* sheep!" *Whap!*

You want to pull the whole uncommitted, hard-hearted flock together and tell them in so many words that they should straighten up and get with the program! You want to discipline them using whatever measures are necessary until they fall into full conformity to your every idea and intention. You go to sleep at night mulling over the obvious source of every difficulty you face: you got stuck with a flock of slacker sheep.

Many years ago, our small-groups pastor came storming into my office fuming about the lack of response to a group-leaders' retreat his team was hosting. They had hoped for hundreds to attend, but only a fraction had signed up. I asked him how the reality made him feel, although I already knew the answer.

"It makes me want to deck every small-group leader out there!" he said. "Why aren't they more committed to this thing?"

"Ah," I said, "so you want to go beat some sheep?"

"Yeah! But they deserve it. I mean, we're doing this retreat for *them*!"

I asked him to have a seat and help me understand a few things. "When did you start marketing this retreat?" I asked.

"Well, the information went out a little late ..."

"Uh-huh. And how much are you charging for it?"

"Well," he said, "we had to raise the cost this year because the hotel we wanted wasn't available, what with the late notice and everything ..."

"Uh-huh. And how far are you asking folks to drive to get there?"

"Well, I guess it's about seventy-five miles farther than last year, but again, it's all because that hotel just refused to bend for us."

"And when is this retreat?"

The small-groups pastor explained that while they'd shot for other options, the only weekend that seemed to work just happened to coincide with our community's spring break, when half the church takes their families to Florida. I recapped his answers for him and then said, "You know what I'm thinking? Based on the facts you've just given me, the sheep ought to beat *you*! This retreat is so ill conceived that I'm shocked *anyone* has signed up."

He thought I had a point.

Throughout my entire ministry, one thing has almost always been true: If I communicate the right mission at the right time of the year in the right way and with the right motivation behind it, the sheep do not disappoint. When I take pains to run down a list of appropriate questions on the front end, I set my sheep up for effective cooperation. Questions like, Is this a good plan? Is it in step with the vision of our church? Have I warmed up this value recently with effective teaching from Scripture? Are my expectations of people reasonable? Have I chosen the right night of the week? Have I communicated effectively? Have I prayed fervently?

Likewise, when I run down that list on the heels of a ministry disappointment, I nearly always discover that it wasn't the sheep's fault — at least not entirely. I find that my idea was ill-conceived or badly timed or poorly promoted or not prayed through with fervency. And I realize that instead

> *Throughout my entire ministry, one thing has almost always been true: If I communicate the right mission at the right time of the year in the right way and with the right motivation behind it, the sheep do not disappoint.*

of reaching for the shepherd's stick come Sunday morning, I must take organizational responsibility instead.

If your sheep aren't responding the way you think they should, put down your stick and ask a few questions first. See if you served your sheep well, because when they're served well, they tend to serve well in return. Never beat the sheep, my friend. A word of loving admonition every once in a while might be appropriate, but put the stick away. Permanently.

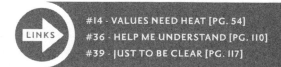

LINKS

#14 - VALUES NEED HEAT [PG. 54]
#36 - HELP ME UNDERSTAND [PG. 110]
#39 - JUST TO BE CLEAR [PG. 117]

personal
integrity

63 | OBI-WAN KENOBI ISN'T FOR HIRE

One of the hottest trends today is the ever-increasing demand for the *M* word. Mentoring—it seems everybody wants it.

Throughout my ministry I've been asked literally thousands of times to be a mentor to someone. On a few occasions, the request came from people who flew from another continent for the sole purpose of waiting by my car in the Willow parking lot to get the opportunity to ask me personally to mentor them.

What concerned me more than their temerity was the expectation behind the question—"Would you be willing to listen to and counsel me, mold me and shape me, direct me and instruct me and hold me accountable? Would you cajole me and encourage me and essentially re-parent me? Would you fill me with your fount of knowledge so that I don't have to search for it myself? Would you, O Great Mentor-to-Be, please serve as my all-knowing, all-sufficient, all-powerful, omnipresent confidant and master, teacher and exhorter, friend and guide, from this day forward, 'til death do us part?"

Truth be told, they didn't really want me. What they *really* wanted, ironically enough, was someone who does not exist—at least not in this realm of life we call nonfiction.

They wanted Obi-Wan Kenobi, the fictional character in Star Wars who was the strong, steadfast, modest, selfless, measured, patient, and wise warrior-wizard whose prowess shaped the fate of an entire galaxy.

"I'll pay whatever you want to charge me!" some would offer. "You just name the amount!"

One basic problem: Obi-Wan Kenobi isn't for hire.

Wise leaders never sign up for unrealistic mentoring arrangements. They spot neediness a mile away and say to themselves, "There is no single human being—especially me, with all my faults and limitations—who is going to be able to meet this person's requirements, so I'm going to do them and me a huge favor and steer clear of this whole deal."

I've developed a practice over the years that has saved me many times from inadvertently falling into the "will you be my mentor?" trap. "I agree that we all need mentors," I say, "and I'm honored that you consider me mentor material. But there are *hundreds* of mentors far more qualified than I, who are ready to assist you! All it requires is that you think about mentoring a bit differently."

I go on to probe what aspects of life they want mentoring in. "Do you need help as a parent or a spouse? Do you need assistance in money management, team building, or goal setting?"

After encouraging prospective mentees to identify their most pressing needs, I try to help them realize that no single individual will be able to serve as expert in them all. "It may take several different mentors to find what you are really looking for," I explain, "but it is possible, as long as you're willing to think creatively about how to enlist mentorship aid."

For example, it's possible to be mentored by someone you've never met. From a leadership standpoint, I've been mentored by the likes of Lou Gerstner and Jack Welch, yet I've never so much as shaken hands with either one of them. I've gone to hear Welch speak, I've watched him host Q&A sessions on TV, and I've read everything he has written. But in terms of having one-on-one time with the man, I never have and probably never will. Still, I consider him a mentor, and I am a far more effective, strategic, and team-oriented leader because of his extraordinary input into my life.

Spiritually, I have been mentored by a bunch of dead guys. Some of the great theologians of the past, like Abraham Kuyper and C. S. Lewis and Dietrich Bonhoeffer, have helped me make monumental progress in my walk with Christ via their books and sermons. The men themselves are long gone, but their mentoring influence lives on in my life. How cool is that?

I meet many leaders who complain that the reason they're still struggling with their

> *I meet many leaders who complain that the reason they're still struggling with their leadership is that "nobody will mentor them." I have little patience for this line of thinking, and I make my position well-known by encouraging them with a few words of compassion, like, "Move off dead center and go get what you need!"*

leadership is that "nobody will mentor them." I have little patience for this line of thinking, and I make my position well known by encouraging them with a few words of compassion, like, "Move off dead center and go get what you need!"

It's limiting to believe that the only way mentoring works is by hovering over a Bible with someone or by sitting across the table from an expert at a restaurant for three hours a week. That said, you don't have to rule out the lunch-date thing altogether. I'd just be *very* careful how you approach it.

Over the years, when I've faced specific challenges that I couldn't overcome on my own, I'd seek out people in my relational sphere who could lend a helping hand. For example, the best dad I've ever known was a man at Willow named Jon Rasmussen. Whenever I struggled to sort out fathering issues, I'd give Jon a call. Four or five times a year, he'd pick up his phone and hear, "Jon, I'll take you to lunch if you'll let me ask you a few questions. I'll keep it short, my friend, but I could really use some insight here."

Another Willow guy was a personal finance whiz. Whenever I had important money decisions to make, I'd do the same thing—buy him lunch in exchange for a little hard-won wisdom.

Still another was a health nut. When I felt I needed a new workout regimen or a better eating plan, I sought counsel from this guy. His help has been absolutely invaluable to me.

This approach is also how I met the former chairman of Motorola, Bob Galvin. Motorola's global headquarters is situated six miles from Willow's campus, and I knew that the success the company had enjoyed for the previous three decades was due largely to this man's leadership expertise. His was wisdom I sorely needed, given the dilemmas in my lap. I called him up and said, "I will buy your lunch if you will answer three very specific leadership questions for me. No strings attached. No back-end pen-pal stuff. Just one lunch, three questions, forty-five minutes tops. I won't waste your time, I assure you."

He agreed. And in large part because I neither wasted his time nor became a pest, he has offered his help to me many times since. These days, when an aspiring leader approaches me with the same parameters and intentionality, I am much more inclined to offer my help as well.

There's no quicker way to repel an accomplished leader than to beg him or her to be your own personal wizard. Ditch the Obi-Wan dream and instead seize creative opportunities to learn from a distance from thousands of mentors who have a wealth of wisdom to share. Then, from time to time, make a reasonable request from a wise person for a very specific kind of input, and your mentoring needs will be met and maybe even exceeded.

#65 - LEAD WITH ALL DILIGENCE [PG. 190]
#68 - READ ALL YOU CAN [PG. 196]
#72 - WE NEED US ALL [PG. 203]

64 | WHAT LIFE ARE YOU WAITING FOR?

Many years ago I shared a conference stage with Joni Eareckson Tada. She did a Q&A session following one of her talks, and someone in the audience asked her how she kept going—how she kept leading and serving and creating—despite her obvious physical challenges.

I'll remember her answer for a long, long time. She said, "This is the only time in history when I get to fight for God. This is the only part of my eternal story when I am actually *in* the battle. Once I die, I'll be in celebration mode in a glorified body in a whole different set of circumstances. But this is my limited window of opportunity, and I'm going to fight the good fight for all I'm worth."

Joni got it right at the conference that day, and I came away from the event more resolute than ever that if I'm waiting for some other life to be courageous, then I'm kidding myself. Through her response, Joni proved that she gets what daring decision-making is all about. She knows how to live life so tuned in to the Holy Spirit that his voice merges with her inner voice; his view of the world becomes her view as well. She has learned how to drown out fear's whispers in favor of adopting God's take on any given situation. She not only knows the right thing to do; she actually *does* it.

A friend of mine who is a high-impact leader called the other day. He is facing a serious challenge but knows exactly what God is asking him to do to solve it. My question seemed patronizing, but that wasn't my intention. "So why don't you do what God is obviously asking you to do?"

He thought for a second and then responded with this: "I just don't want to lay it on the line one more time."

I understood what he was saying. It happens to us all.

Leaders fight fear regularly. From time to time it gets the best of them, and leaders who were once willing to do God's bidding no matter how risky become overly circumspect and start playing things safe. Don't let it happen to you: this is your one and only life!

In my opinion, risk in ministry is riskier than risk in any other field, including the business world. Most of the time, corporate leaders are just betting money. And despite appearances, the stakes are actually quite low where only money is involved. Obviously, losing a few thousand or a few million isn't all that fun, but at the end of the day, it's still just money.

Church work introduces vastly more valuable currency, because in church work you're dealing with God's reputation and the eternal souls of real people. These sky-high stakes — as well as the steeper consequences for getting the whole deal wrong — add up to a very visceral experience when church leaders set about the task of assessing risk. After all, what leader in his or her right mind wants to be the one to screw up a "God-thing"?

It's a fear I understand all too well.

Around Willow's twenty-fifth-anniversary mark, our senior leaders made plans to pursue three very ambitious goals. We would launch three regional campuses, undertake a hundred-million-dollar building expansion, and fund international ministry projects totaling an additional five million dollars. And we'd do all three things at once.

I stayed in contemplation mode longer than usual because in my view there was a high probability we could fail in all three areas. If we failed in the launch of our regional campuses, that failure could reflect poorly on a reputation it had taken a quarter century to establish.

The other two initiatives elicited equally fearful feelings. To our knowledge, no local church had ever done a building campaign on the scale we were planning. And *everyone* knows that "international ministry projects" are to be avoided like the plague.

It could all go terribly wrong. We might wind up oh-for-three and squander millions of kingdom dollars in the process. Not exactly the level of hope and optimism you'd expect from a leader, right? I knew what I ought to do, but I also knew there would be push-backs and complications, frustrations and surprises. Did I really want to lay it all on the line ... again?

In moments like those, I had to jolt myself into a heightened state of awareness by asking, "Has God spoken clearly to me on this faith step? Has he spoken to the team members around me affirmatively? Then step up, Hybels! What life are you waiting for?"

This is the only leadership life I get, my one and only shot at following God the way I feel him prompting me to do so. This isn't some pregame warm-up. It's the *game*, and the clock is ticking!

What life are you waiting for?

It's one of my favorite mantras. And it's hereby on loan to you.

This is the only leadership life I get, my one and only shot at following God the way I feel him prompting me to do so. This isn't some pregame warm-up. It's the game, and the clock is ticking!

LINKS

#6 - BOLD MOVE [PG. 32]
#44 - THE BIAS TOWARD ACTION [PG. 134]
#71 - I'D NEVER DO THIS FOR MONEY
[PG. 201]

65 | LEAD WITH ALL DILIGENCE

You've probably had the experience of sitting by a window on a commercial airliner during a nighttime flight. The beverage cart and pretzel packages have come and gone, you're sick of staring at a laptop screen, and eventually you find yourself, forehead pressed against the side glass, utterly captivated by the vast reaches of darkness below.

After a few moments, vaguely, faintly, you make out the lights of a little village or a city in the distance that cut through the expanse of blackness. "I guess there is life down there after all," you think. Perhaps you feel the same sense of relief I do in those moments, relief that communities of light exist, if for no other reason than to keep all that is dark from dominating the scene entirely.

Sometimes I look at our local, national, global landscape and wonder if the shadows of human depravity will forever obscure the view. But then, just when it seems everything is destined for darkness, a fragile flicker of light punctuates the view. In that particular place, malevolence gets pushed back one step or two. Something evil gets resisted. Something good gets lifted up. That which is right, reclaimed. Pure, unadulterated hope gets ignited once more.

Today there is hope to be found in our families. There are families in places all around the world in which things are really going well. Moms and dads are working out their loving relationships in healthy and functional ways. Kids are being raised up in a God-honoring environment. Family flickers are coming to life.

There is hope to be found in our churches. Many are executing important plans inside their four walls, but they're also transforming their communities. There is hope in our businesses. Some are building quality products, enhancing the lives of their employees, and turning a profit while they're at it. There is hope in our neighborhoods, where people are pulling together and applying their best creative solutions to the problems they face. Social movements are forming around large-scale trouble that imperiled an entire generation. What a difference these efforts will make!

Wherever you see something going well—whenever light begins to chase back the darkness that threatens to engulf our world, look closely. There stands a leader who is holding that candle.

It's certainly true at Willow. Whenever something is going well around our church—and some things are going *really* well these days—it only takes a few questions to figure out which leader is behind the uprising. Likewise, find something that is in disarray around Willow, and you'll probably learn that there's a leadership crisis at the center of that difficulty.

It all boils down to diligent, God-honoring leadership. It's true for Willow, and it's true for your church. It's true for your family, your business, and your community. Leaders must "lead with all diligence," Romans 12:8 says (my

> *Wherever you see something going well—whenever light begins to chase back the darkness that threatens to engulf our world, look closely. There stands a leader who is holding that candle.*

paraphrase). And throughout history, when evil needed to be confronted or when oppression needed to be resisted, when slavery needed to be abolished, when governments needed to be overthrown, when churches needed to be rejuvenated, when major social movements needed to be started, one such "diligent" leader stepped onto the scene.

They would communicate the vision for change.

They would commit personally to paying the high price of leadership.

They would roll up their sleeves, release their best energies, and pursue the vision with everything they had. And at the end of all their efforts, a flicker of light would stand tall, light that pushed back the darkness one millimeter more.

All progress hinges on diligent leaders, God's preferred method for transforming the world.

LINKS

#7 - AN OWNER OR A HIRELING [PG. 34]
#72 - WE NEED US ALL [PG. 203]

66 | To the Core of My Being

What do you believe in, to the very core of your being? If a particular issue elicits a passing opinion but not your most passionate activism, if it raises your curiosity but doesn't rile you up enough to do something about it, if it pricks your consciousness but wouldn't prompt you to take a bullet, then it's not a core-of-my-being issue. But if it sets off a seismic shift in your inner person that you can feel from the top of your head to the bottom of your feet, then you've got a core-of-my-being issue on your hands.

If I'm preparing to confront a values violation within our ministry or an injustice out in the world, I ask myself whether this is something I feel to the core of my being. I think through whether I'll be able to live with myself if I don't take action. If I determine that I won't be able to sleep at night or face myself in the mirror, I act. And I do so passionately! I express my beliefs, give voice to my concerns, and let the chips fall where they may.

I believe when God gives someone the gift of leadership and commissions them to lead something, he also places a few core-of-my-being issues on that leader's heart. And I'll just bet that if you grabbed a journal and a pen and devoted an hour to the task, you could come up with yours right now.

What are the values or convictions that you feel to your toes? Maybe they were born of Bible study. Maybe they showed up on the heels of pain. Or perhaps they are the result of a Holy Spirit prompting

What are the values or convictions that you feel to your toes? Maybe they were born of Bible study. Maybe they showed up on the heels of pain. Or perhaps they are the result of a Holy Spirit prompting intended just for you. Sort out what they are, communicate them to those you lead, and then live according to them as you exercise your ministry leadership.

intended just for you. Sort out what they are, communicate them to those you lead, and then live according to them as you exercise your ministry leadership. Let those issues arbitrate key decisions. Let them tell you where you throw your time and energy and passion and money. And let them help you stay close to the vision God is asking you to pursue.

LINKS

#7 - AN OWNER OR A HIRELING [PG. 34]
#73 - EXCELLENCE HONORS GOD AND INSPIRES PEOPLE [PG. 206]

67 | ALWAYS TAKE THE HIGH ROAD

When I was in my early twenties, I served as one of the youth leaders for a group called Son City. We had grown from a whopping attendance of twenty-five people to more than a thousand in less than three years, and God was rocking the house! Students were finding faith in Christ, mindsets were shifting, and lives were being transformed. But the church we operated in was in a difficult era. They had gone a long time without a senior pastor, the new pastor they brought on board struggled to rally any interest in his vision, and at least a portion of the adult population filled their spare time by resisting everything our student ministry stood for.

It was in the midst of this set of dynamics that God called me to leave that ministry and start Willow in a rented movie theater.

The new senior pastor of the church and I agreed that I would draft a resignation letter and then read it to the entire congregation on my final Sunday morning. So I immediately started putting together my thoughts, including my frustration with the deacons, my disappointment with the board of trustees, and my not-so-humble perspective on just how incompetent the entire church staff seemed to be.

The week before I was to read my resignation letter, one of the older men in the church took me to lunch. He thanked me for the impact Son City had had on his daughter's life and then asked me what I planned to say when I addressed the congregation. I told him of my plan to shoot *really* straight and explain exactly what was broken in the church and how frustrating it had been to try to build a strong youth ministry in a weak church. The more I talked, the more a very concerned look overtook his face.

"Is this a bad approach?" I asked before I had even finished reading him my notes.

His response is one I'll never forget. He said, "Bill, I cannot urge you strongly enough to take the high road on Sunday. Bless what you can bless.

Thank everyone you can thank. Cheer on what is appropriate to cheer on. And be done with it. I am an old man now, and never once have I regretted taking the high road."

> "Bless what you can bless. Thank everyone you can thank. Cheer on what is appropriate to cheer on. And be done with it."

I left that meeting, but his words never left my mind. When it came time for me to stand before the congregation and read my letter—the one I wrote after I ripped up the first one—I did take the high road. I admitted the wrongs I had done. I asked for forgiveness for the rookie errors I had made. And I blessed the church for being the kind of place where a gathering of a few dozen clueless kids could become such a meaningful, wide-reaching ministry. My departure caused a fair amount of upheaval, but less than two years after my decision to leave to start Willow, the leaders of that church invited me back to speak at their annual banquet. Which never would have happened had I proven myself a low-road guy.

Throughout Willow's history, there have been scores of times when staff members have misbehaved or underperformed and ultimately decided to leave. Something in me desperately wanted to climb up to the rooftop and shout, "I want you all to know this was *their* fault! Sure, they resigned, but only because they knew they were about to get *fired*!" So often I have wanted to say my piece, defend my honor, and protect our church from miscreants-in-the-making who might be listening from down below. But then I'd hear that elder's exhortation float through my consciousness. "Bless what you can bless. Thank everyone you can thank. Cheer on what is appropriate to cheer on. And be done with it." And so, with the Spirit's help, I would.

Proverbs 22:1 says that a good name is more desirable than great riches and that to be esteemed is better than silver or gold. But the only way to get that good name is by taking the road that most honors God, that most blesses people, and that leads to healthy and functional relationships long into the future. The truth I was given is the truth I give to you now: "I'm an old(er) man now, and never once have I regretted taking the high road."

LINKS

#29 - SPEED OF THE LEADER, SPEED OF THE TEAM [PG. 94]
#76 - FINISH WELL [PG. 214]

I had a meeting years ago with a senior leader at Willow who had been suc-cessfully leading one of our largest departments for a long period of time. She asked for the meeting because she said she was facing a leadership crisis and needed help. She was a very good leader, but the size and scope of her responsibilities had increased threefold in a short period of time, and she was caving under the perceived pressure she felt from all that change.

I listened intently as she described her issues. For twenty minutes straight, I listened. But then my patience wore thin. I stopped her mid-monologue and said, "I'm sorry to interrupt, but the conundrums you've noted in our conversation so far are all Leadership 101 issues. Yet you're a 501- or 601-level leader. Let me ask you a question: What are the names of three leadership books you've read in the last twelve months?"

She couldn't think of one.

"It's confounding to me," I continued, "that you could be entrusted with scores of staff members and hundreds of thousands of resource dollars, yet you feel no compulsion whatsoever to read books to improve your leadership. The brightest, godliest leaders on the planet have written fantastic content on the very same issues you're wrestling with, and it's only an Amazon-dot-com click away. One click!"

The conversation further confirmed what I have long believed: far too many leaders in high positions of responsibility neglect their need to read.

The older I get and the longer I lead, the wider my knowledge gap becomes and the more aware I am of all that I don't know about leadership. But then there's Romans 12:8, which says that I am to "lead diligently." How am I supposed to lead diligently when there is so much left to learn?

Leaders have a responsibility before God to *constantly* get better, and one of the most reliable ways to do so is to read. Great leaders read frequently. They read voraciously. They read classics and new releases. They soak up lessons from the military, from academia, from politics, from nongovern-mental organizations, and from church leaders who are leading well. They refuse to let themselves off the hook in this regard, because they know that all great leaders read.

When you read, you invite new information into your subconscious mind. You may spend ten full hours going cover to cover and at the end feel like you're none the wiser. But then a day or a week later, you face a leadership dilemma that you are able to solve only because you read that book.

> *Leaders have a responsibility before God to constantly get better, and one of the most reliable ways to do so is to read.*

Just last month I was walking through an airport, about to board a three-hour flight home. It was the perfect amount of time to plow through the four sailing magazines I had tucked in my briefcase. "Perfect!" I thought just as I passed a bookstore. Feeling a pang of guilt, I thought about the weeklong vacation I'd just enjoyed with my family. I thought about the challenges that were facing me back at Willow. And I realized I owed my team that three-hour window of preparation so that I could lead as effectively as possible once I was home.

I stopped into the shop and picked up a business book on making wise decisions. It was so captivating that I underlined at least a third of it on my trip home. Not surprisingly, many of the dilemmas I faced that week required every ounce of new knowledge I had gleaned from that book. Just imagine if I had settled for sailing magazines!

I have little patience with leaders who get themselves into leadership binds and then confess that they haven't read a leadership book in years. If you're a serious-minded leader, you will read. You will read all you can. You will read when you feel like it, and you will read when you don't. You will do whatever you have to do to increase your leadership input, because you know as well as I do that it *will* make you better.

LINKS

#60 - PAY NOW, PLAY LATER [PG. 174]
#65 - LEAD WITH ALL DILIGENCE [PG. 190]
#73 - EXCELLENCE HONORS GOD AND
INSPIRES PEOPLE [PG. 206]

69 | LEAD SOMETHING!

I'm often asked how, in addition to reading, to get better as a leader. And if I'm in a playful mood, I'll sometimes say with a smile, "Just *lead* something!"

Leaders get better when they are on the job, engaged in the day-to-day rigors of trying to push a ball up field. They get better from getting a little banged up and determining to keep going anyway. But the best way for leaders to get better is to lead something besides their "main thing."

I believe church leaders get better when they serve on boards that have nothing to do with the churches they serve. "Serve a local bank, serve your neighborhood YMCA, serve an interesting NGO, serve a community college," I coach leaders, "but find a leadership opportunity that is complex, diverse, and consistent with your passions. The carry-over effects will astound you!"

When I was invited to serve on the World Vision board in the mid-1990s, the organization was facing some difficult challenges. We were attempting to raise and direct hundreds of millions of dollars toward starving children in more than one hundred countries around the world—no small task.

The complexity of the situation stretched me and often kept me up at night. It catalyzed an intense period of research and reflection. But more than anything else, it *prepared* me. My board experience there set me up for the challenges at Willow in ways I could not have imagined, because as God opened the doors for our church to cross continents and hire language translators and take our ministry into scores of international venues, I felt equipped in ways that I never would have without having served on the World Vision board.

Later I would lead a sailboat racing team. And although the implications of our decisions weren't nearly as consequential as those we faced at World Vision, many of the lessons I learned by leading nine crew members in national-caliber regattas found their way back to my role at Willow.

Think about it this way: if you are a distance runner who runs six times a week but never engages in any other physical activity, you could play a single game of touch football and think you were absolutely going to die. Likewise, if you run and play football but never lift weights, eight reps of bicep curls could leave you begging for mercy. When you use different muscles, you force your body to flex and develop in new ways.

Leaders must invite the same type of cross-training into their leadership development regimen.

The more varied the environments in which you exercise your leadership gift, the stronger that gift will become. Lead something besides your main thing. You will become a far more effective leader.

> *The more varied the environments in which you exercise your leadership gift, the stronger that gift will become.*

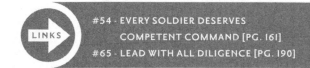

LINKS

#54 - EVERY SOLDIER DESERVES COMPETENT COMMAND [PG. 161]

#65 - LEAD WITH ALL DILIGENCE [PG. 190]

70 | ARRIVE EARLY OR NOT AT ALL

Jesus said to let your yes be yes and your no be no.[21] So when I say yes to meeting with a group of my colleagues at a certain time and place, I do everything in my power to keep my word. Promptness is about character, and leaders are not beyond the rules that govern things like courtesy and character.

When a leader says to a group of direct reports, "I'll be at the restaurant at noon to meet with the four of you," all four of those people want to know whether that leader will in fact keep his word. If the leader strolls in fifteen minutes late, the team members who likely broke their backs to get there on time feel devalued.

But when a leader factors in traffic and detours and last-minute incoming calls and *still* manages an early arrival, the team members feel affirmed.

Within leadership circles around Willow, if people do encounter a complication that makes them late for a meeting, the first thing they do upon arriving is to apologize. No excuses; just a sincere "I'm sorry." Anyone can give a valid reason why they're running a bit behind. But it takes grace

> *Promptness is about character, and leaders are not beyond the rules that govern things like courtesy and character.*

and relational intelligence to keep that reason at bay until you've first let the group members know that their feelings rank higher than your justification.

When I've had to issue an apology like that, my whole team relaxes in response. They are reminded that I really do value their time, I really do view them as equals, and I really do want my yes to be yes.

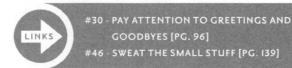

LINKS

#30 - PAY ATTENTION TO GREETINGS AND GOODBYES [PG. 96]
#46 - SWEAT THE SMALL STUFF [PG. 139]

I'd Never Do This for Money

More than twenty years ago I took my first ministry trip to India. The hotel that had been arranged for me was awful. The bed was so filthy that instead of tossing back the covers and jumping in, I threw open my suitcase and removed every stitch of clothing I had packed. I stretched out polo shirts and slacks and every other available garment so that not one inch of my mattress could be seen. Sounds paranoid, I know, but whatever insects were crawling all over my bed that night warranted it.

I awakened the following morning and felt like I was stuck in a bad dream. The heat, the smells, the density of people, the open sewers, the dead animals—it was more than I could take. And that was *before* my opening talk.

The translator I used had never translated before, I couldn't see my notes in the dim lighting, no one seemed to get fired up about the Acts 2 vision I was casting, and the entire day felt like a massive waste of time, energy, and passion.

I got back to my hotel room that evening, kicked off my shoes, fell backward onto my bed, and shouted loudly enough for the whole hall to hear, "Who needs this?"

The rats on the floor looked up at me as I sank further into despair. "I am a suburban Dutch guy from Barrington, Illinois," I thought. "What in the world am I doing here? And why do I keep signing up for stuff like this?"

Back at Willow, on more occasions than I can count, I've climbed into my car in the church parking lot after a late-night meeting that seemingly yielded nothing in terms of progress and spent the entire drive home asking myself if the

There isn't enough money in the world to motivate me to do what I do. But there is a kind of compensation that does fire me up. It's God's commendation to all his sons and daughters who serve faithfully: "Well done."

kingdom dream was really worth the effort. After a weekend of services where I preached three times as passionately as I know how, and then greeted hundreds of people who wanted to talk about their pain and struggle only to arrive at home to receive an email from a key staff member informing me that he is moving to another church, I silently repeat the question from the hotel room in India: "Why do I sign up for this?"

In moments like these, the admittedly odd way I remind myself that God's vision is worth my best energy and ongoing faithfulness is to say, "One thing is for sure: I would never do this for money!" Call me crazy, but this axiom works for me. The phrase reminds me that God is the one calling me to live this life, and I want to be found faithful one day. Truth be told, there isn't enough money in the world to motivate me to do what I do. But there is a kind of compensation that does fire me up. It's God's commendation to all his sons and daughters who serve faithfully: "Well done."

In 1 Corinthians 15 the apostle Paul says that if there is not a resurrection and if there are no eternal rewards, then why don't we all just eat, drink, and be merry? "If I fought wild beasts in Ephesus for merely human reasons," he continues, "what have I gained?"[22]

When leaders have a quick and succinct way to check their motivations during times of trial in ministry, they stand a far better chance of enduring over the long haul. Refreshing my conviction that I would never serve so wholeheartedly for money helps me stay clear on why I do serve with my whole heart. God alone has my ultimate allegiance, he is the direct object of my highest affection, and his promises are what I'm banking my entire ministry and eternity on.

LINKS

#7 - AN OWNER OR A HIRELING [PG. 34]
#20 - THIS IS CHURCH [PG. 68]
#56 - SPEED VERSUS SOUL [PG. 166]
#65 - LEAD WITH ALL DILIGENCE [PG. 190]
#72 - WE NEED US ALL [PG. 203]

72 | We Need Us All

By vocation, the translator I use when I minister in Germany is a success-ful dentist. In addition to having built one of the most highly respected dental practices in Frankfurt, he has a great family who all love God.

For many years, he and his family were part of a dying church. They watched sixty members dwindle to forty, then forty dwindle down to twenty-five. Attendance finally leveled off with a handful of faithful people who were desperate to keep the church alive.

Several years ago while he was translating one of my talks on leadership, something clicked in his mind. He went home that night and prayed to God. "God has given me leadership gifts that I have used to build a thriving dental practice and a thriving family," he later said of his revelation, "but I've never considered using that leadership capability to help build a thriving local church!"

He paid a visit to the remaining members of his church's board of direc-tors. "It seems to me that our candle has all but gone out. But I believe God has given me some leadership gifts, and I wonder if there's something I can do to try to turn this situation around a little."

"Go for it!" the board members said. "If there is something you can do to help out, then do it!"

He began to do what leaders naturally do. He asked tough questions of the people in charge: "Why are we doing this? What's our mission? What's our focus? What's our strategy? What are some strengths we can build on?"

And he asked one critical question of everyone else: "Will you help? Will you help? Will you help?"

He formed a few teams and led them diligently until the church was back on track. Slowly but surely, their numbers rose. Thirty, then forty-five, then fifty, then sixty. He helped ensure that the pastor they eventually hired possessed leadership and teaching gifts.

On a recent trip to Germany, after a long day of speaking engagements (for us both!), I sat with him in a restaurant until just after midnight and learned his church is now running a hundred and sixty people every weekend. They have undertaken a building addition, God is changing lives, and the future looks bright.

I was congratulating him, telling him how proud I was that he had taken a portion of his leadership octane and used it to better the local church, when I noticed his head hanging low. I stopped talking for a moment and waited for his eyes to reconnect.

"Bill," he said, "it has been harder than I ever thought it would be. There have been so many times when I just wanted to quit. Honestly, it was a lot easier to build my dental practice than it is to build this church."

I nodded, thinking, "I know exactly what you mean."

He kept going. "But you know, when I slip into those dark periods, I sense God saying, 'You're doing great! And I'm here to help.' He carries me. He heals me up and sets me back on course. Each time, I find I'm able to go just a little farther down the road."

"I really appreciate what you're saying," I replied. "And I can certainly relate to the dynamic you describe."

The apostle Paul knew the dynamic well too. During what was probably the deepest valley of his leadership, when he had been betrayed and abandoned and left for dead, Paul says in 2 Timothy 4:17 that "the Lord stood at [his] side."

No one else would stand by Paul's side, but God came near. God stood beside him. God carried him. God empowered him. And then the light of morning broke through.

On any given day, I can look around Willow and find strong leaders who serve our church exceptionally well. But I can also find some who are on the ropes. Had I been present during my German translator's darkest nights of the soul — those times when he admittedly was on the ropes — I would have said to him the same words I often have to say to myself, based on themes I love in Scripture: "Lean into the empowering presence of God and realize that you're not alone. Reach out to God, and he will reach out to you. He will restore your soul. He will encourage you and inspire you. He

"Lean into the empowering presence of God and realize that you're not alone. Reach out to God, and he will reach out to you. He will restore your soul. He will encourage you and inspire you. He will heal you up and set your feet back on course. He will rally other leaders to your side who will pray for you and walk with you."

will heal you up and set your feet back on course. He will rally other leaders to your side who will pray for you and walk with you. He will remind you that nothing that you do for him is in vain. Nothing."

We need us *all*, my friend, whatever it is we are leading, wherever it is on the globe. The kingdom advancement we're pursuing needs us all.

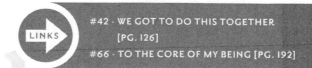

LINKS

#42 - WE GOT TO DO THIS TOGETHER [PG. 126]
#66 - TO THE CORE OF MY BEING [PG. 192]

73 | EXCELLENCE HONORS GOD AND INSPIRES PEOPLE

Years ago during a speaking engagement, I stayed in a hotel in Dallas. It was late at night, and after flipping channels for a while, I landed on ESPN, which is how I learned that tennis legend Martina Navratilova had just won a grueling match in Florida earlier that day. I drifted off to sleep.

The next morning, I got up early and headed to the hotel's gym. It was barely five thirty when I stepped onto the indoor track, but I wasn't the only one there. A woman was coming through the double glass doors. It was Martina Navratilova. She'd been in Florida the day before, she was in Dallas now, and she was up at the crack of dawn, eager to hit balls back and forth in a hotel gym as if she had nothing better to do. Like sleep.

It's just a guess, but I don't think anybody told her to do this. I think she crawled out of bed and pulled on workout clothes before the sun was even up because of an insatiable inner need for excellence. She wants to win *that* badly.

Leaders in every arena possess an internal quality-control mechanism, a longing for excellence that won't let them off the hook. It pushes them to achieve higher levels of effectiveness and efficiency than anyone else would ever hold them accountable for. Mine was born many years ago after I spent time reflecting on a single passage in the Bible.

> *Leaders in every arena possess an internal quality-control mechanism, a longing for excellence that won't let them off the hook.*

In Malachi 1:6 God tells the people of Israel that he has an offense against them. Their minds race as they try to figure out what they've done wrong; finally, they ask for some clarification: "Well, what did we do?"

Speaking on God's behalf, the prophet Malachi responds, "What did you *do*? You *know* the laws about making sacrifices. You *know* that you ought to go out into your herds and select the best, most valuable, most prized lamb from your flock for your offering to God. But instead of doing what you know to do, you are heading out to your fields and intentionally overlooking the top sheep in the herd. Rather than selecting your prized lamb, you look for one that's sick and blind and lame and leaning against the fence, ready to keel over! You grab *that* one and race for the altar before it dies, thinking, 'It'll suffice. It's only for God.'"

Malachi then said to the people, "This is what God says. 'Don't even *bother* building a fire. Don't waste your time. I don't want the sick and lame and blind and almost-dead lamb. What a mockery to me! Either bring me the prized lamb or bring me nothing at all!'"[23]

Can you imagine receiving a rebuke like that directly from God? I read the passage that afternoon all those years ago and felt as though something had permanently shifted inside of me. The Spirit of God seemed to be saying to me that everything I do in Christian leadership—every plan I put together, every meeting I lead, every talk I give—needs to be my best lamb, my very *best* offering! Not so that I'll operate out of paranoia or wild perfectionism, but so that I'll live from my heart's deep desire to honor God.

In my thirty-plus years as a senior pastor, nobody has ever set a standard for me to try to reach with regard to my preaching. It would be a waste of their time, because my internal standard will always be higher than that which others can mandate. People at Willow have had to tolerate a lot of pretty sorry sermons, but at those particular times in my life, those talks were the best ones I could give.

I wonder what would happen to every church on the planet if every pastor, staff member, volunteer, elder or deacon, and servant in children's ministry were to say, "You don't have to worry about me. I'm committed to giving my best lamb, every single day. I'm going to live in vital union with God, and I'm going to consistently render my most excellent offering. The standard I have established is higher than any you could possibly set for me!"

What would happen to our leadership? What would happen to our preaching? What would happen to our music? What would happen to our administrative functions if *everybody* in the church established their own level of quality control based on the excellence of Jesus Christ and remained dogged in their determination to honor him with their best every time?

We must fight for excellence because it is excellence that honors God. It is excellence that inspires people. And it is excellence that means trouble for the enemy of our souls.

#44 - THE BIAS TOWARD ACTION [PG. 134]
#46 - SWEAT THE SMALL STUFF [PG. 139]

74 | ADMIT MISTAKES,
AND YOUR STOCK GOES UP

D on't make it seem like a big project, okay?"
These were the last words I heard from a Willow Creek board
member just before I headed into weekend services to preach. The year was
1977, and the "project" he was referring to was the establishment of Willow's
new campus in South Barrington. We had purchased a piece of land, we had
approved a construction plan, and after two long years, finally we would be
moving into a permanent location.

This astute board member knew that the press would try to nab me for
an interview after the worship service, and he wanted to be sure I didn't
overstate our intentions and throw our development plan into a state of jeop-
ardy with the members of our community. If I went down the wrong path
from a communications standpoint, all of our progress could be brought to
a screeching halt.

Immediately following the service a reporter cornered me and asked, "So,
Bill, what are your plans out there at Barrington and Algonquin roads?"

In a total lapse of judgment, I compared the campus we envisioned to
Woodfield Mall.

Woodfield Mall is a 2.2-million-square-foot shopping center in nearby
Schaumburg, which today boasts more than three hundred upscale shops
and hosts more than thirty million shoppers a year. Not exactly the best
association to put in this reporter's brain.

"We have put a *lot* of thought into this," I explained in my most helpful
tone, "and we want to have a *huge* auditorium and *lots* of classrooms and
adequate offices and a *very nice place* where we can treat people who have
counseling needs and ..."

I went down the long list of our dreams as if impressed with my ability
to remember them all. This guy really had me going! Yeah ... going, going,
gone.

It wasn't until the drive home that the troubling reality of my situation hit me. "It's exactly what the board member told me not to do, but did that stop me? Nooo! I can't believe what I've done!"

Would I call the board member to confess my gross misstep, or would I let him discover the news in the next morning's paper? Walking ten feet across my living room to where the phone sat had never seemed so hard. I made the call.

After exchanging pleasantries, I said, "Listen, when you read one particular article in tomorrow's paper, you may have homicidal thoughts form in your mind. You told me very specifically to watch out for reporters, but I got myself tangled up in a conversation with one, and in the end, I just caved. I got all excited about our building program and said far more than I should have said. I'm terribly sorry. This will never happen again."

He saw the article the next day and called immediately. With classic dry wit, I think his exact words were "Way to low-key the building program, Bill."

As horrible as that experience was, it actually represented significant progress on my part. For the first couple of years, my leadership mantra had been "Prove thyself." I spent inordinate amounts of time and energy trying to prove to the board, my colleagues, and my direct reports that my leadership could be trusted. I wanted those to whom I was accountable to believe that my batting average was high with regard to making wise decisions to the point that when I made an unwise one, my reflex reaction was to hide it for as long as possible. I was afraid my stock would go down, my superiors would trust me less, or both.

One time when I was faced with a particular hiring choice, I said, "Look, I know this person is on the younger side, but I'm going to entrust the role to him. I think if I coach him and train him, he'll become good over time."

The job wound up being way too big for him, but instead of confessing my poor decision, time and again I'd look my colleagues in the eye and say, "I think he'll come around. Just give it more time." He never came around.

Once during a fund-raising effort, it became apparent that as a leadership team, we were a long way from achieving our agreed-upon goal. Instead of revealing the truth, I bluffed my way into garnering time extensions and then had to scramble behind the scenes to figure out how to get more money from folks. Not good.

I now know just how important it is for leaders to shoot straight as soon as they realize they've screwed up. When the president of an institution I'm on the board of steps up and admits an error or gives a timely warning regarding initiatives that are not going as planned, I do a deep exhale. In that moment of truth, I think, "As your board of directors, we stand ready to help you. We're going to rally around you and prove that together we can find a way out of this. Thanks so much for admitting the truth!"

Maybe all leaders have to fall prey to and suffer the consequences of the "hide it and they'll never know" approach before they wake up and realize that they can't hide it forever and that "they" will always know. Each time senior leaders shift the blame—someone *else* dropped the ball, someone *else* is at fault—their credibility plummets with every single person who knows the real deal. When something goes wrong, board members, staff members and other onlookers want to see which leader will take responsibility for it. *That* is the leader they will respect. That is the leader they will follow.

Admitting your mistakes says something profound about your basic integrity as a leader. "I took a risk here and thought it would turn out a certain way, but it didn't. It's my fault. You were probably more objective about this situation, yet I didn't take your advice. I didn't heed your counsel, and I'm very sorry."

These are the words of a trustworthy leader.

> *Admitting your mistakes says something profound about your basic integrity as a leader.*

#50 - DON'T SCREW UP [PG. 150]
#52 - FACTS ARE YOUR FRIENDS [PG. 155]
LINKS

75 | FIGHT FOR YOUR FAMILY

According to 1 Timothy 3:12, one of the qualifications of a church leader is that you manage your household well. If you don't get that right, then you probably won't get your responsibilities in leadership right either. Show me a leader who can cast a white-hot vision and who builds great teams and who does great things for God but who has a bitter spouse and disillusioned, cynical children, and I'll show you trouble waiting to happen.

The first leadership test I have to pass every day, every week, and every month is that of leading my family well. Am I casting a positive vision for my family, and am I inspiring them? Am I bringing about events that build unity among them? Am I communicating effectively and solving problems at home?

> *Leadership's first test is the test of the family, and it's the test that must be passed before any further tests may be taken.*

Leadership's first test is the test of the family, and it's the test that must be passed before any further tests may be taken.

In my twenties, I fell into the trap of being flattered by my followers' constant request for my presence. I wanted to be needed and thought it was exceptionally affirming when staff offered to go sailing with me, go running with me, have lunch with me, drive me to the airport, and walk me to my car. Any fifteen-minute slot they could get, they'd take. And I willingly gave it.

Eventually it began to dawn on me that if I kept saying yes to every request, these people would suck me dry! I started saying, "You do realize I have a family, right?"

Of course they realized this. And at some level all of them cared. But the urgency and the importance of the ministry situations they faced overshadowed their concern for my family time. They needed my participation to push their initiatives forward, and so they put the onus on me to protect family time. "I know Bill is devoted to his family," they'd reason, "so if he needed time to be with them, I'm sure he would take it. But I'm going to keep asking for his time until he says no."

I woke up very slowly to the fact that nobody in my organization was going to fight for my family but me. I am not saying anything bad about my colleagues or my congregation. They are the best! But I have to fight for time with my family. I have to fight to show up in decent emotional shape every time I walk through the front door of our home, I have to fight for family vacation time, and I have to fight to integrate them in my ever-increasing travel schedule. In these examples and a thousand others, when it comes to my family, the one and only fighter is me.

When that became clear, I decided not just to fight but to fight *hard*. In the early days, I found that to be a great dad, I needed to be home four nights a week. So six months out, I'd block four nights a week on my calendar for family time. People would vie for those evenings and I'd say, "I'm so sorry, but I have a prior obligation."

My kids are both adults now. They love God, they love the church, they love being together as a family, and I love the fact that God has rewarded my fights this way. That first generation went pretty well, but I have a grandson now, and I am having to sign up for another season of fighting for him. With God's help, this battle will be won as well.

No matter how Christian or collegial your work environment may be, in the rough-and-tumble battle for organizational progress, what's always needed is more of the leader. More of your time, more of your resources, more of your support, and more of your involvement, regardless what it costs you to give it. On most church calendars, it is never convenient for the senior leader to be gone. Your presence is required during capital campaigns, major transitions, holiday seasons, and seemingly every moment in between. Before you know it, you're expected to be omnipresent.

So a piece of hard-won advice: Buck the system. Observe your Sabbath. Take your time off. Max out your vacation days. Drag your kids on ministry trips with you. And never look back. When it comes to your family, the only one fighting for it is you.

LINKS

#56 - SPEED VERSUS SOUL [PG. 166]
#58 - CREATE YOUR OWN FINISH LINES [PG. 169]

personal integrity | 213

76 | FINISH WELL

In forty years of employment, I've left only three organizations. First was my father's produce business, followed by the AWANA organization. Then later, I'd leave my job at South Park Church in Park Ridge, Illinois, in order to start Willow Creek.

The most difficult departure of these three was from South Park, where I had to say goodbye to a thousand high school students and the entire adult congregation. Another lesson I learned from the man who told me to bless whatever I could bless as I departed South Park was that how I left an organization is how I would always be remembered there. If I finished well, then I would be remembered with admiration and my contribution would forever be looked on with favor.

I've never forgotten that advice.

It is the nature of organizations that people come and go. So in the early days of my leadership at Willow, I decided to hold up "finishing well" as a key value. "The question is not whether we'll leave," I'd tell my colleagues. "The question is how *well* we'll leave when it's finally our turn to go."

I gave a few parameters to the staff to make sure we were all on the same page regarding the way departures should occur. "Finishing well means telling your supervisor when you sense restlessness creeping in," I explained. "It means that when you begin to feel frustrated in your role here, you invite your boss into the discussion.

"Finishing well means that if you secure employment arrangements with another organization, you stick with *this* organization until it is appropriate to go. You engage with your boss in crafting a reasonable transition plan so you don't leave a gaping hole during a very critical season. You help explain to the organization why you're leaving in constructive terms so that confusion

> *"The question is not whether we'll leave," I'd tell my colleagues. "The question is how well we'll leave when it's finally our turn to go."*

and bad stories don't emerge, which would wound those of us left in your wake. You invite your colleagues who have grown to love and respect you to honor you adequately! And you insist on working diligently until the final sixty seconds of your employment.

"You do everything you can do to leave on a positive, life-giving note so that your legacy here is a God-glorifying one."

I often coach leaders that the time to teach their staff about finishing well is *not* when things are in a state of organizational chaos. The time to teach on it is when things are cruising along nice and smooth. Devote an entire staff meeting to the benefits of finishing well and preserving a good name.

When you uphold the value of finishing well, departures tend to lose their drama. Someone will come into your office to tell you they have been called by God to serve elsewhere, and instead of reaching for the panic button, you'll say, "How can I serve you? Have you thought about the timing of this? What do we need to do to help make sure you finish well?"

A pastor I know told me recently that although he had taught on the concept of finishing well, he never thought he'd actually have to apply it in the context of his leadership role. But one day his worship pastor came into his office and said he was taking a position in another church. As if that news weren't bad enough, he added that his first day on his new job needed to be the Sunday before Easter.

My friend balked at this worship pastor's plan. "You're leaving one week before Easter, when we host the biggest worship arts production of our entire year? The production *you're* in charge of?"

I smiled as he told me this story, glad to know someone else dealt with stuff like this. "What wound up happening?" I asked.

"I asked the worship pastor if he remembered a staff meeting we'd had last year," my friend continued, "where all of us who said we'd agree to one day finish well raised our hands and joined in a prayer of commitment. He said that he did remember that meeting and that he also remembered raising his hand.

"I then asked him if he believed that leaving our church seven days before his most significant annual contribution would equate to finishing well, and he said no, he guessed finishing well would necessitate a different course of action."

That worship leader came full circle after that conversation. He agreed to stay another month and see the Easter production through to its successful completion. Things are still in motion for this particular transition, but every indication points to the worship pastor finishing really, really well. Good for him!

My son, Todd, also had to face the issue of finishing well recently. He and a friend decided to quit their jobs, buy a boat, and sail around the world. The plan would require Todd to leave a position he had enjoyed for five years on Willow's staff, but once the boat had been purchased and the water began calling, he was eager to get going.

He went to his supervisor and explained his desires. His supervisor said, "Todd, if you can stay through Memorial Day and keep going really strong until this year's ministry season is over, our team would release you with happy hearts."

Todd had to dig deep to live that out. He put in fifty to sixty hours a week for more weeks than he'd originally intended, but over a family dinner at the end of it all, he looked across the table at me and said, "Dad, it feels really great to finish well." I was proud of him.

Someday you will finish the assignment God has you pursuing right now. Someday I will as well. My sincere desire is that both of us will finish well for the sake of the One who called us and sustained us all the way to the end.

LINKS

#14 - VALUES NEED HEAT [PG. 54]
#67 - ALWAYS TAKE THE HIGH ROAD [PG. 194]

ACKNOWLEDGMENTS

Ashley Wiersma, who has ably assisted me with several other creative projects, had a clearer vision for this book than I initially did. When I finally saw how helpful this approach could be for developing leaders, I caught the fire. (Thankfully, Scott Bolinder did too.) With infectious enthusiasm, Ashley linked arms with Paul Engle, Bob Hudson, Rob Monacelli, Ben Fetterley, and others from Team Zondervan whose considerable passion and proficiency made these efforts seem more like recess than homework. Collectively, we sensed guidance from God each step of the way — an invaluable gift that gave cohesion to our team and meaning to our work.

NOTES

1. Bill Hybels, *Holy Discontent* (Grand Rapids: Zondervan, 2007).
2. http://www.billygraham.org/mediaRelations/bios.asp?p=1.
3. Acts 21:13, author's paraphrase.
4. Acts 21:14, author's paraphrase.
5. 1 Timothy 5:18.
6. The article "Intelligence Unit's Livability Ranking" (*The Economist*, August 2007), part of the *Worldwide Cost of Living Survey*, assesses living conditions in 127 cities around the world by looking at nearly forty individual indicators grouped into five categories: stability, health care, culture and environment, education, and infrastructure.
7. 1 Corinthians 4:16.
8. From 1 Corinthians 13:1–7.
9. Catherine Johnson, *Lucky in Love: The Secrets of Happy Couples and How Their Marriages Thrive* (New York: Penguin Books, 1992), 63.
10. Nancy credits author Roger von Oech with the original "umbrella" concept, in his book *A Whack on the Side of the Head* (New York: Warner Books, 1983).
11. http://headlinehistory.co.uk/online/East%20Midlands/World%20War%202/A%20War%20Begins/story571.htm.
12. http://www.stanford.edu/group/King/popular_requests/frequent-docs/birmingham.pdf.
13. Steven B. Sample, *The Contrarian's Guide to Leadership* (San Francisco: Jossey-Bass, 2002).
14. Ephesians 6:12.
15. Matthew 11:30.
16. Mihaly Csikszentmihalyi, *Flow: The Psychology of Optimal Experience* (New York: HarperPerennial, 1991).
17. Tom Clancy, *Into the Storm: A Study in Command* (New York: Putnam, 1997).
18. See Matthew 10:28.

19. Jack Groppel, *The Corporate Athlete* (Hoboken, N.J.: John Wiley & Sons, 1999) 27–28.
20. See Matthew 16:26.
21. Matthew 5:37.
22. 1 Corinthians 15:29–34 NIV.
23. Malachi 1:6–14, author's abridgment.

WILLOW CREEK ASSOCIATION

This resource is just one of many ministry tools published in partnership with the Willow Creek Association. Founded in 1992, WCA was created to serve churches and church leaders striving to create environments where those still outside the family of God are welcomed—and can more easily consider God's loving offer of salvation through faith.

These innovative churches and leaders are connected at the deepest level by their all-out dedication to Christ and His Kingdom. Willing to do whatever it required to build churches that help people move along the path toward Christ-centered devotion; they also share a deep desire to encourage all believers at every step of their faith journey, to continue moving toward a fully transformed, Christ-centered life.

Today, more than 10,000 churches from 80 denominations worldwide are formally connected to WCA and each other through WCA Membership. Many thousands more come to WCA for networking, training, and resources.

For more information about the ministry of the
Willow Creek Association, visit: **willowcreek.com**.

The Power of a Whisper

Hearing God.
Having the Guts to Respond.

Bill Hybels

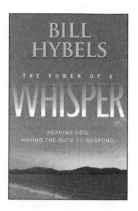

"Without a hint of exaggeration," says pastor and author Bill Hybels in his new book, *The Power of a Whisper: Hearing God, Having the Guts to Respond*, "the ability to discern divine direction has saved me from a life of sure boredom and self-destruction. God's well-timed words have redirected my path, rescued me from temptation and re-energized me during some of my deepest moments of despair."

In *The Power of a Whisper*, vision is cast for what life can look like when God's followers choose to hear from heaven as they navigate life on earth. Whispers that arbitrate key decisions, nudges that rescue from dark nights of the soul, promptings that spur on growth, urgings that come by way of another person, inspiration that opens once-glazed-over eyes to the terrible plight people face in this world — through firsthand accounts spanning fifty-seven years of life, more than thirty of which have been spent in the trenches of ministry, Hybels promotes passion in Christ-followers' hearts for being wide open to hearing from God, and for getting gutsier about doing exactly what he says to do.

Just Walk Across the Room

Simple Steps Pointing People to Faith

Bill Hybels

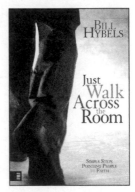

What if you knew that by simply crossing the room and saying hello to someone, you could change that person's forever? Just a few steps to make an eternal difference. It has nothing to do with methods and everything to do with taking a genuine interest in another human being. All you need is a heart that's in tune with the Holy Spirit and a willingness to venture out of your "Circle of Comfort" and into another person's life.

Just Walk Across the Room brings personal evangelism into the twenty-first century. Building on the solid foundation laid in *Becoming a Contagious Christian,* Bill Hybels shows how you can participate in the model first set by Jesus, who stepped down from heaven 2,000 years ago to bring hope and redemption to broken people living in a fallen world. Now it's your turn. Your journey may not be as dramatic, but it can have a life-changing impact for someone standing a few steps away from you—and for you as well, as you learn the power of extending care, compassion, and inclusiveness under the guidance of the Holy Spirit.

The stakes are high. The implications are eternal. And you may be only a conversation away from having an eternal impact on someone's life—if you will just walk across the room.

Available in stores and online!

Holy Discontent

Fueling the Fire That Ignites Personal Vision

Bill Hybels

What is the one aspect of this broken world that, when you see it, touch it, get near it, you just can't stand? Very likely, that firestorm of frustration reflects your holy discontent, a reality so troubling that you are thrust off the couch and into the game. It's during these defining times when your eyes open to the needs surrounding you and your heart hungers to respond that you hear God say, "I feel the same way about this problem. Now, let's go solve it together!"

Bill Hybels invites you to consider the dramatic impact your life will have when you allow your holy discontent to fuel instead of frustrate you. Using examples from the Bible, his own life, and the experiences of others, Hybels shows how you can find and feed your personal area of holy discontent, fight for it when things get risky, and follow it when it takes a mid-course turn. As you live from the energy of your holy discontent, you'll fulfill your role in setting what is wrong in this world right!

Available in stores and online!

Share Your Thoughts

With the Author: Your comments will be forwarded to the author when you send them to *zauthor@zondervan.com*.

With Zondervan: Submit your review of this book by writing to *zreview@zondervan.com*.

Free Online Resources at
www.zondervan.com

Zondervan AuthorTracker: Be notified whenever your favorite authors publish new books, go on tour, or post an update about what's happening in their lives at www.zondervan.com/authortracker.

Daily Bible Verses and Devotions: Enrich your life with daily Bible verses or devotions that help you start every morning focused on God. Visit www.zondervan.com/newsletters.

Free Email Publications: Sign up for newsletters on Christian living, academic resources, church ministry, fiction, children's resources, and more. Visit www.zondervan.com/newsletters.

Zondervan Bible Search: Find and compare Bible passages in a variety of translations at www.zondervanbiblesearch.com.

Other Benefits: Register to receive online benefits like coupons and special offers, or to participate in research.

ZONDERVAN.com/
AUTHORTRACKER
follow your favorite authors